"Garage sales are the lifeblood of a budget-minded, creative room makeover, and shopping them is an art unto itself. *Garage Sale Gourmet* has all the info you need to turn yourself into a garage sale pro. Go forth and shop well!"

— Joan Steffend, Host of *Decorating Cents*
Home & Garden Television

"What sets this book apart is the way it takes me step by step through the process of becoming a garage sale gourmet myself. It covers loads of useful information and street-tested tips, and it's written in an easy, conversational style that makes me feel like I'm sitting around chatting with the authors. Whether you're a novice or a garage sale veteran, this book can help bring new levels of creativity to your home."

— Lisa Winick, Artist and designer

Garage Sale Gourmet

Garage Sale Gourmet

Anita Chagaris
Randy Lyman

Streetwise Shopping for Fun, Profit, and Home Improvement

Fighting
Words Press

P.O. Box 1041, Oakland, CA 94604

Garage Sale Gourmet
Streetwise Shopping for Fun, Profit, and Home Improvement
© 2005 by Anita Chagaris and Randy Lyman

Published by Fighting Words Press
P.O. Box 1041, Oakland, CA 94604

Cover and interior design by Pneuma Books, LLC
visit www.pneumabooks.com for more information

Publisher's Cataloging-in-Publication Data
(*Provided by Quality Books, Inc.*)

Chagaris, Anita.
    Garage sale gourmet : streetwise shopping for fun, profit, and home improvement / Anita Chagaris, Randy Lyman.
      p. cm.
      Includes index.
      LCCN 2004114210
      ISBN-13: 978-1-933181-21-9
      ISBN-10: 1-933181-21-4

    1. Shopping--Handbooks, manuals, etc. 2. Garage sales--Handbooks, manuals, etc. I. Lyman, Randy. II. Title.

TX335.C38 2005   381'.195
                     QBI04-200467

10 09 08 07 06 05   6 5 4 3 2 1

For our family

Table of Contents

Part 1 The Recipe for Success

Like charity. So be charitable toward yourself. Before you go anywhere, sit down and take a close
look at where you live, and see not just how your
home looks now, but how you dream of it. Then
we can talk about how to begin systematically
turning your visualization into reality. We'll also
go over one of the most important — and overlooked — things to do before you leave the house.

In some neighborhoods you can drive around
and follow the signs to a dozen garage sales in a
single morning. But you'll use up a lot of gas —
and time — and of course this strategy doesn't
work everywhere. That's why it's important to
plan your garage saling days. This small investment of time will save you time on the road,
not to mention wear and tear on your car and
your nerves.

Yes, you can go garage sale shopping without
bringing anything — but why? You'll only wish
you had. We'll go over what to tote along for in-
specting your potential purchases, wrapping
them, carrying them, and getting them home.
Even a few simple items, like newspapers and a
tape measure, can make you a more confident,
capable shopper and the whole experience much
more effective and enjoyable.

We finally hit the road and talk about some simple strategies for zeroing in on the garage sales
most likely to have what you're looking for. Some
things you can anticipate, but you can learn more
than you'd think in the five seconds it takes to
drive past a front yard. We'll also talk about the

basics of negotiation and how you can get the best deal possible without fancy footwork, just by keeping a few tips in mind.

Part 2   Home Cookin'

If all you're buying is kids' clothing or a toaster, you only need to know that it fits or works. But if you're collecting, say, a particular style of china, then a bit of research can help you recognize pieces when you see them. Sometimes you'll want to do research before you buy a piece, but often you won't be able to until after you've gotten it home. We'll discuss how to do both.

You probably won't stumble across many genuine antiques at garage sales, but you can find collectible items that, even if not worth a fortune, can make your home look like a million bucks. In this chapter we'll go past the basic research strategies to learn how you can locate hard-to-find pieces — like that one missing sugar bowl in your table service — by looking where other people don't think to look.

Some people shop at garage sales intending to buy cheap so they can resell for more on eBay or at their own garage sales. We'll go over some tips for holding your own garage sale, but more importantly, we'll get to the heart of being a garage sale gourmet — and that's the satisfaction of turning dust into gold, of repairing and refinishing your purchases simply and creatively to redecorate a room or your entire house for a fraction of the cost of buying new furnishings. Even better, the final look will express your personal style and give you a sense of accomplishment and creativity that store-bought furnishings can't give.

Here are some addresses, URLs, phone numbers, book publishers, and other resources to help you on your garage saling journeys. There's also a checklist of garage saling supplies to go along with chapter 3.

In the intro

Introduction: Assume the Position

When my sister-in-law Denise and I get to a garage sale, especially if it's a big one with lots of stuff that seems interesting (which we can pretty much tell from the car), we sometimes look at each other and say, "Ready? Assume the position!" Then we round our shoulders like hunchbacks and start giggling hysterically. And then we attack.

The position — more commonly known as shopper's hump — is where you'll find yourself if you spend entire days at garage sales like we do, bent over table after table examining old jewelry and other small things; and that's why keeping in shape — or at least keeping your shoulders and neck from cramping — is important. So stretch and exercise. But let's discuss why you'd make a life out of garage saling in the first place. No, you don't have to become misshapen addicts like me and Denise, but by garage saling just a few hours a week, you can make big changes in the quality of your life at home.

Why Garage Saling Makes Sense

We live in an age of junk. I know, because a lot of it's in my house. Probably yours too. To me, though, it's not junk at all. Somebody threw away an old ceiling light; I got the welds fixed, spray-painted it, and now my hallway has something that shines even when the lights are off. Someone else dumped some ratty old chairs, and now I have a nice set of four around my dining table, painted glossy white with re-covered seat cushions (the padding was in perfect condition). I got the table at a garage sale too, but not the same sale, and also a small shelf for the wall beside it, and the mirror above the shelf. The scented candles on the shelf I bought at an upscale boutique, once I had a nice place for them. Except for the candles, I decorated the entire room from garage sales.

Someone's throwaway was just what I needed — that's what millions of people all over the country say every weekend. Whether you call it a garage sale, yard sale, tag sale, white elephant sale, or anything else, everywhere the concept is the same: some people try to sell their "junk" while other people buy it and call it treasure — or at least "just what I needed for my living room."

It's an underground economy, in a way; resale goods are no longer looked down upon as secondhand (see sidebar "Secondhand Rose") but have become popular — and even fashionable. People pay thousands of dollars for the shabby chic look.

For a growing number of people who can't afford the real economy any more, the world of garage sales, flea markets, thrift stores, and other secondhand venues has become a regular place to shop. It makes sense. These places can stretch the family budget a long way. Who can afford to buy everything new these days, when the cost of raising two kids is more than what two parents earn? When a college education requires a lifetime of savings? When your fixed income doesn't stretch as far as your bills any more? When gas, food, DVDs, and all the nickel-and-dime expenses of daily life — no matter how old you are — start adding up to a lot of nickels and dimes?

While saving money is the benefit most people associate with garage saling, what they don't realize is that it can be a fun lifestyle as well. Garage sales are for the budget watcher and bargain hunter, but also for those who'd like to express their individuality in the way they live. Trimming your costs doesn't mean you have to cut the quality of your life. If you know what to look for at garage sales, how to look intelligently, and how to refinish what you buy with a few simple touches, you can create a nice home environment and a sense of personal style and accomplishment at the same time. You can save money without it becoming a major personal sacrifice. You can be a bargain hunter and a life artist too. This is something you can't buy in a department store.

I've been garage saling for more than twenty years. Garage sales are where I bought most of the furniture in our current house and where I found a large part of the three thousand-piece Snoopy collection I began when I was nine years old. In our last house, I completely redecorated my daughter's room from garage sales, as well as the master bedroom, the living room, and dining room. In this book, we'll talk about how you can do the same thing.

How This Book Can Help You

Many people who say they would never go to garage sales really start to like it once they try it. Maybe that's you. Most of my friends that I've turned into garage salers wouldn't go near one at first, not even get out of the car. But then one day they'd tell me, "Guess what I did this weekend? I went garage saling!" It can get addictive once you see what's out there. Some of you may already be avid garage salers, but now you'd like to kick your habit up to the next level.

Holding your own garage sale is a good, fun way to clear out your home, and a successful sale can net you hundreds of dollars. But it's also something you do maybe once or twice a year, because who's got the time and energy to hold a sale more than that? In fact, some cities prohibit you from

Secondhand Rose

Buying secondhand no longer carries the stigma it once did. Au contraire. The National Association of Resale and Thrift Shops estimates that the number of thrift, consignment, and resale shops is increasing about 5 percent a year. According to the NARTS website (www.narts.org), "Resale will continue to gain popularity and become an even more important segment of the retail industry. Word of mouth is constantly spreading the value and excitement of resaling as a fun, easy and friendly shopping option. Today's shoppers are savvy. Years ago, during the era of 'conspicuous consumption,' some liked to boast about how much they paid for something... today's consumer brags about how little they paid for something! Today's shoppers are also environmentally conscious, making recycled clothing and furnishings a hot commodity."

holding more than two, otherwise they consider it a home business requiring a business license, which can have an impact on your state and federal income taxes. There may be other regulations too: New Jersey, for instance, requires you to purchase a state-sanctioned garage sale kit. A successful sale requires a lot of advance planning and preparation and will take up most of your weekend.

Garage sale shopping, on the other hand, is also fun, but you can do it as often as you'd like. The hundreds of dollars you save on furniture, toys, appliances, decorations, and so forth, will feel like extra money earned all year long, without the IRS knowing or caring. Successful shopping requires some planning, but you can do it in a couple hours

Friday evening and then enjoy the rest of the weekend. In the end, you'll have an attractive, interesting, livable environment that you created yourself — one that you can keep on creating as your needs and fancies change.

That's what this book is about. Together, we'll cover step by step how to:

- Figure out what you want
- Look for it intelligently
- Plan a day or weekend of garage saling
- Pack the essentials for handling any situation
- Redecorate your home with flair
- Hold more profitable sales of your own by learning how a garage saler shops

Whether you're a beginner, a veteran, or somewhere in between, this book will take you further along your garage saling journey by exploring ways to save money and transform your home.

Types of Garage Sale Shoppers

What kind of garage sale shopper are you? Are you a bargain hunter? A collector looking for specific items? A college student getting by on financial aid? A couple furnishing your first home or buying toys and clothing for your kids? Retired? Or do you just like living a nonconformist lifestyle? Do you intend to shop regularly? Or just for seasonal things, or for a specific move or other purpose?

Before you go anywhere, it helps to know exactly who you are and what you expect from garage saling. Let's look at some of the types of garage sale shoppers I've met out there.

Beginners
Recognizable from a distance, they're the ones gingerly picking up clothing from a pile while the more experienced plow through it. They handle dusty things like they're crystal, afraid to touch them. They're always asking how much things cost instead of making an offer.

Bargain Hunters
If your garage sale starts at nine, someone always shows up at seven, while you're still setting up and probably still waking up. They may apologize for showing up early but then ask if it's okay to look at your stuff before the opening, offering some lame excuse why they just can't make it during the two whole days you're actually holding the sale. That's because their real goal is to grab all the good stuff before anyone else sees it, especially bigger ticket items like furniture, which can be refinished and resold fairly easily at a high profit margin. You can see the trucks and vans of bargain hunters loaded with tables and chairs by eight, by which time they've clearly hit a few not-yet-open garage sales already.

Regulars
They go to every sale they can, not necessarily looking for anything in particular, but to do the circuit with their

thermos of coffee, hoping to find that one special thing they need, knowing and accepting (especially collectors) that they're not going to find something every week. They come out to meet people, to get some fresh air and exercise, and often find sales by following the signs around their neighborhood.

Working Parents

That would be me and my husband Lou. It's hard to justify spending a lot of money on nice furniture when you have young kids. They'll have their friends over and it's going to get trashed, scuffed, spilled on, you name it. Garage sale furniture you can simply repaint or recover without worrying about the item's price, since a $20 chair plus paint is still cheaper than a $200 chair. As a garage sale gourmet, you can afford to keep a stylish home that's kid-friendly without looking like the kids have taken possession.

Budget Watchers

Well, who doesn't need to watch their budget? That includes all the other types of garage salers (and you can be more than one). You don't need to give a reason for wanting to save money. The nice thing about garage saling is that getting good deals can be fun too, as you get outside, talk to people, and see how imaginative you can get for how little. Garage sales let anyone break out of life's routines and trust its unpredictable richness.

Myths and Misconceptions

Most people don't buy everything new anyway. Ever bought a used car? Garage saling is no different. If you've never done it, however, you might be holding onto some notions that have kept you from doing it. But these notions, like the song says, ain't necessarily so. Let me help you get over them.

- "Stuff at garage sales has all been used."

  So has everything in your house. At a garage sale, it's merely someone else's house. You don't know who used something before, or where it came from, but why should that matter? Especially with porcelain, glass, or silverware, which can simply be washed. Clothing can be dry cleaned. Maybe it's not "used" after all; maybe the seller bought an item and then never got around to taking it out of the box. I buy clothing with the tags still on it all the time. How is this different from buying at a department store? In the department store you can't afford it, but at a garage sale you can cash in on people's lazy shopping habits and changes of mind. Once you see your bargain shined up and used in your own home, the feeling that it's always been yours sets in very quickly.

- "Stuff is dirty."

  If you're that freaked out over dirt, bring rubber gloves, then wash your purchase when you get it home. How dirty can it really be? Thoughtful sellers (and even most thoughtless ones) will clean up their merchandise at least a little bit, believing, correctly, that people tend to pay more for nicer looking items. Besides, do you think the toys you buy will stay clean once your own kids have them? Instead of worrying about items being dirty, bring a pocket-sized bottle of anti-bacterial hand wash and an extra bottle of water. You might want to freshen up after handling a lot of things, but it's all just dirt and dust. It comes off.

- "I can get what I want online."
  That's right, you can. You can also wait weeks for it and pay tax and shipping, not to mention higher prices if you get caught in an eBay bidding war. I'm not talking about things like books and CDs, though you can find those at sales too; I mean the things you'd go to garage sales for, like furniture and appliances. You don't bid at garage sales, except rarely, when someone else is interested in the same item. Garage sales are about impulse buying and getting your hands on the goods immediately and inexpensively, an experience online shopping can't offer. Garage saling also gets you away from your computer screen and out into the fresh air and your community, where you'll find actual people instead of pixels, so you get to know your neighbors and the neighborhood instead of the usual faceless mall crowds.

- "I can't find what I want at garage sales."
  Eventually you will, if you keep at it. Just as often, what will happen is that you'll find the perfect thing accidentally, something you probably didn't even know you were looking for until you found it. That's the magic of garage saling. Learn to trust it.

- "It's too time consuming."
  Going to the mall or grocery store is time consuming too. Garage saling should be fun, not a chore. The amount of time you spend at it depends on how badly you want to save money and redecorate your home nicely. It's not something you have to do every week-end. Most garage sales are over by late afternoon, so it's not like you're sacrificing a whole day. Garage saling should enhance your quality of life in the doing, not just the getting.

- "I'm no good at negotiating."
  That's what sellers say too. Most of the time, you won't even realize you're negotiating. Besides, it's not like negotiating nuclear weapons treaties; we're talking about a few dollars for lamps and chairs. Truth is, most people don't know how much to sell their belongings for, so they may be just as intimidated by the negotiating process as you are. There's often little to negotiate. You wouldn't believe how many times I've asked how much someone wants for an unticketed item, only to hear them say, "I don't

know," or turn to the seller next to them to ask. If they quote more than you want to pay, you can always say thank you and walk away. If an item is ticketed at $10, ask if they'll take eight. Most likely they just want to get rid of it and $8 will sound great. Negotiating is not hard.

Final Words before We Head Out

Your tastes in clothing and furnishings can and will change over time. You won't think shabby chic is cute forever, or maybe the modern pieces you have now will start to seem sterile and plastic. Perhaps you move into a home or apartment with a whole different set of rooms, or more rooms, that catch more light and reveal just how ratty or stuffy your old furnishings really are. Or maybe you don't move but simply get tired of looking at the same furniture in the same place year after year, gradually wearing out. In other words, home decorating is not something you do once and then you're done for life; it's a part of living every day and every phase of your life. By doing your decorating at garage sales, you can make your home environment as unique and changeable as you and your family are — and do it as often as you want without it costing a fortune.

If you've never been serious about garage saling, I hope you'll catch some of the enthusiasm that I and millions of other people experience every weekend. If you are a

Room with a View to Savings

Here's an example of how you can decorate a room nicely by shopping just at garage sales and resale stores. Let's look at everything I bought for my daughter Chloe's bedroom.

- Bed frame at a garage sale: $10.

- Chandelier from a Las Vegas flea market: $40. I repainted it, rewired it, and bought crystals for another $60.

- Wardrobe from a thrift shop: $180. I spent a lot more than I usually would have because I really liked the piece, although it needed new knobs ($60) and paint ($20, but it's the same paint as the bed frame, so I spread out that cost.)

- Rolltop desk: $75 at the Salvation Army store.

Now go out and price all this stuff new. We saved so much on these and some other minor items, like curtain rods, that we were able to put more money into the big ticket items we wanted, like Chloe's bedspread and a custom-made sofa for the living room, which I also furnished from garage sales.

garage saler, then you already know what I mean. The new life you make may be your own. Let's get out there. Assume the position!

Part One
The Recipe for Success

In this chapter

1

Garage Saling Begins at Home

"Hold on, kids!" I shouted as I whipped the car around.

By now my kids are used to their mom acting like a crazy woman. So they gripped the arm rests and braced themselves as I did a quick check for traffic and hung a fast one-eighty in the middle of a quiet suburban block near my house. There was a garage sale, and something at the curb had caught my eye as we drove past.

There were so many garage sales in our old neighborhood in Venice, California, that I never had to plan ahead if I wanted to go garage saling in the vicinity. Our house was surrounded by huge tracts of homes and apartment buildings, and someone was always moving. In an area like that, there are at least a couple of garage sales nearby every weekend. My new neighborhood, a few miles away in Santa Monica, is better; I can visit a dozen sales before noon just by following the signs tacked up on trees and telephone poles.

If you shop at garage sales infrequently or only in your neighborhood, you probably don't need to spend much time planning out your shopping day. Actually, I come across some of my best finds by accident — sometimes when I'm not even shopping. But if you shop frequently or out of your area — or want to expand your shopping horizons to new areas — then good planning is a must.

We'll devote the next chapter to planning your shopping trips, but there are things to plan and think about before you even leave home. They come down to this: You need to figure out what you're looking for, where it's going to go in your home, and how you're going to get it there. That's in this chapter.

Taking Stock

Sometimes when I'm out garage saling, I'm not looking to buy anything in particular; I just want to go window shopping. I never know when something will unexpectedly catch my eye. Two minutes ago I didn't know it existed, and suddenly I just can't live without it. But then I struggle within myself: Should I spend the money? Maybe I can talk the price down. Where am I going to put it? Do I need it? Oh, but it's so cute....

Trusting in the miracle of the unexpected is one of the greatest joys of garage saling. But if you're trying to create a look for your home, you also need to think about what you want, and the way to start is to look closely at what you already have.

Sometimes when I have quiet time to myself, like when the kids are at school or at a friend's house, and maybe I'm in the middle of gathering up laundry or other chores, I stop what I'm doing, sit down in one of the rooms of my house, and just look around. I let my eyes roam over the whole room — the walls and furniture, the clothes and toys lying around, and into the closets — and I take note of what needs to be done. Sometimes it's merely repairs: this baseboard needs to be patched and repainted, that chipped switch plate needs to be replaced, those curtains need a new tieback.

But mostly I dream about how it all might look, what each room needs to become a pleasant place to hang out, a room to live in, not just occupy. I do this just about every time I'm in my kids' rooms, because their need for space changes rapidly as they grow. My seven-year-old daughter Chloe needs more room for clothes, while Alex, age eleven, needs a new desk, with room for a computer so he can study and download music. In each room I look around and think something like this: Chloe's old nightstand needs to be tossed, Alex's walls would look good in a deep sky blue, this corner of the living room needs something decorative like a basket or a free-standing candle holder. This is easy to do when you're relaxed, and it's also a good way to get relaxed: taking yourself out of the daily rush of chores and work and family demands for a few minutes to let your thoughts and imagination drift. It's not something you finish in one sitting; you'll see more each time you do it.

I get up and go through the closets. Chloe will scream if I get rid of this dress, I tell myself, but she outgrew it last year. I love my miniskirt outfit, but I keep pulling it out of the closet and putting it right back in because I never have an occasion to wear it. Lou's long-sleeved shirts are getting frayed at the collar. By doing this, I get rid of some things and see what else we need. There's no reason to keep an old outfit just because I think it might come back in style; it might not. But if it does, I'm bound to see another one I like better. Whatever I pull out of the closet goes to Goodwill, unless I'm planning my own garage sale, in which case I'll keep it stashed away until then.

You get the picture. Do tasks like getting rid of old clothing right away so you don't have to think about them again. Make a list of minor repairs and touch-ups to follow up with later. You can organize this list by room and take care of one section of your home or apartment at a time. Or break it down by task — painting, repairing, replacing — and then do all the painting, repairing, or replacing in all rooms at once so you don't have to keep switching from one set of tools to another. Either way, the change will be noticeable and you'll have completed something just by taking it in bite-sized segments.

Go through your home systematically this way, one room at a time: the kitchen, bedrooms, living room, bathrooms,

Garage Sale Gourmet

laundry room, home office, and even the garage. Take note of which furniture or accessories you want to keep and which you'd like to get rid of. The process is the same if you live in an apartment, except that you probably have fewer rooms and the list of repairs goes to your landlord.

Look around, notice, dream, clear things away, and start writing things down. And keep your lists. You'll want to refer to them again.

Dreaming Your Dream House

I'm the kind of person who always has a sense of what kind of look I want to create, even if I don't know right away exactly how to create it. I do know that I can change the whole look of a room just by altering a few details, maybe by adding or painting an item or two — that is, by changing a few inexpensive accessories, something I can do easily at garage sales. If my furnishings were based on expensive room sets from department stores, this would be much more difficult.

The challenge for me then is to find the pieces that will work together to create the look I want. I wanted to do Chloe's room in shabby chic, with a lot of antiqued white.

Tip!

Don't be afraid to imagine — or put — colored paint on the walls instead of something safe, like white or eggshell. A colored background can give a whole new look to your current furnishings. And don't overlook details either. Sometimes just changing the little things, like drawer handles or a floor lamp, can be enough to get a look or theme going.

She has a small room with only one window, so not only is a light color scheme important, but I had to consider how to use the wall space effectively, something most people don't think about. I thought tall, slim pieces would work best. I figured this out by sitting quietly in her room and visualizing it in different ways.

A small room forces you to be really creative, especially a child's room, because you can't just spread things around. You have to cram a lot into a small space without it feeling cramped, providing room for play and homework while making it all accessible and safe. You don't want your little daughter pulling her hundred-pound dresser on top of herself while reaching for her socks in the top drawer. A simple L-bracket will secure a tall dresser to the wall, but you'll want to take this into account in your planning, not in the emergency room.

Looking around your rooms might not always be enough. You might be new to all this and not have a good idea of the possibilities. That's why home decoration magazines exist and earn millions of dollars through advertising. Look through them to give yourself ideas. Read the articles and photo captions too; they explain the rationale behind certain looks or arrangements, which can suggest new ways of thinking about your own living space. Cut out pictures or articles with looks that you like and keep them in a file folder. Start thinking about ways to create the same effects without paying their advertisers' prices. In time this will start to come naturally, especially once you're out at the garage sales. The more you feed your mind with ideas, the more you'll start generating your own.

This is where serendipity comes back in. Sometimes you might not have a clear idea of what you want in a room even after looking through the magazines, but then you stumble across a table or dresser, love it at first sight, and it becomes the inspiration and focal point for the exact look you didn't know you wanted. "That'll look perfect by the living room window," you'll say, and I can almost guarantee that from then on, you'll keep running across other things for the living room that match it or complement it in some way. Explore creative mismatching.

In other words, try to know in advance what you want, but be open-minded when you're at the sales. If you see something you like, chances are you already have a place in your home to put it.

Writing It Down

Once you start thinking about your dream home, it'll be hard to keep track of everything you want, so start writing it all down. This shopping list will be your ally, because it won't be a simple list of items like you'd take grocery shopping, but a detailed information sheet, with all the specs you'll need to determine if an item you like will actually work in your home or wardrobe. If you've organized the fix-it list you made earlier by room, you can now add to it the furnishings that each room needs. Or start a new list.

If I'm looking for, say, a loveseat for the living room, I write down the measurements of the largest loveseat that would fit where I want to put it, which I know because I measured the space. I might note the ideal size too, since I don't necessarily want to fill all the space available. I'll write down particular colors or fabrics I want. If I'm looking for a lamp, I'll write down which room it's for, whether I want a hanging lamp or a floor lamp, and so on. The more you write down, the better you'll be able to find exactly the right thing.

There's no one right way to keep such a list, no standard or "best" format. You can use a pad of yellow legal paper or a spiral notepad that fits conveniently into a pocket or purse. You can organize it into sections by room or type of item (e.g., lamps, nightstands). If you use a home computer for household tasks, like paying bills, set up an Excel spreadsheet with columns for item, dimensions, room, color, top price you'll pay, or anything else that will help you make the right decision out in the field. Before you leave, print an updated list and stick it onto a clipboard with a regular pad of paper as backing. That gives you a system big enough to hold copious notes yet compact enough to carry around.

Your list doesn't have to be just words either. When you see magazine pictures of room styles or individual items that you like, cut them out and make a file to take with you to the sales. Write your own dimensions on the images, along with notes like, "Perfect for the dining room." Take photos of the rooms you're decorating and print them out on plain paper to take with you for reference or upload them to your PDA. If I have them, I'll carry paint swatches of my wall colors (or the colors I'm considering painting the room) so I can match fabrics to them.

Of course, once your friends hear about all this and see what you're bringing home, they'll want you to shop for them as well. So make a new list, or just add to the current one. I find things for my friends all the time because I know what they're looking for, and they find things for me because I'm on their lists. A detailed list is especially important when you're shopping for friends because you need to know not just technical things like measurements and color, but details that are easy to overlook, like how much they're willing to pay. You don't want to buy the "perfect"

Tip!

If your shopping list is an Excel spreadsheet, you can sync it to your PDA so you can keep it with you and make changes to it any time. Most PDAs these days come with pre-installed software that can sync spreadsheets, text files, and even digital photos, so you can see your rooms in much more accurate color than a paper print-out. You can also get sync-friendly shopping list applications that let you enter notes and other information into sortable categories. See "Going Further" at the end of the book for more stuff like this.

$50 dresser for your best friend only to find out she won't pay more than $30. That's why I write down their phone numbers too, so that if I run across a really great piece, I can call on the spot and negotiate for them over the phone. You know what each other's homes look like, so share your home inventories and you can all be on the lookout for each other.

Getting It Home

This sounds like we're skipping to the end, but we're not. Believe me, it's frustrating to pay a good price for a beautiful piece of furniture that you love and then find out it won't fit in your car. You need to find this out before you go anywhere.

You do this by measuring your car. Whether you're driving a huge SUV or a hatchback, you need to know how large a piece of furniture your car can handle, and what shape. I got a good deal on a chair once. I was so excited. It was short and wide, and I figured I could fit it easily into my compact sedan. Instead, I spent nearly half an hour exhausting myself while I knocked off the rearview mirror and nearly ripped the seats and cracked the windshield. Finally, I got it into my front seat, but when I got home, I had trouble getting it back out. A year later I put it out at a garage sale, but when a customer told me it dated from the 1950s and was worth several hundred dollars, I decided to keep it after all. My point, though, is that I almost did $500 in damage for a five dollar chair. Know how big your car is.

Measure every place in your vehicle where you can store things. The trunk or rear cargo area is pretty regular and box-like, not counting the wheel wells, so that should be fairly easy.

It's the backseat that's tricky. Sometimes I thought a piece I'd just paid for would fit because I'd measured the backseat area, but I forgot to remember that a car is not a perfect box inside; it's got armrests, a transmission tunnel, and weird angles. Measure the space in all its dimensions: door to door, seat to ceiling, front of the backseat to back of the front seat, with and without the passenger seat tilted or slid forward.

Measure the front passenger space as well, because a stool or nightstand might fit there if the backseat is full. Measure some diagonals, and the door openings too, top to bottom and side to side, subtracting space for the seat's profile. A piece might fit in your car but you can't *get it in* because the door only opens so far. Finally, put the tape measure down and get a real sense of your car by trying to see which of your own chairs, tables, and nightstands will fit inside it.

Someday you might buy something large, like a dressing table with a mirror, that is obviously not going to fit into your Honda Civic no matter how much you measure it. In this case, ask the seller to deliver. Most of the time they'll be accommodating, especially if they have a pickup or SUV. Remember, they want to get rid of what they just sold you (or could sell you, if you can find a way to get it home); they don't want to store it back in the garage or move it elsewhere. If you show the slightest interest in buying, they're usually willing to help. Chances are they considered this when they put the item up for sale.

One time I drove past a garage sale, but then I changed my mind, made one of my crazy turns, and ended up finding this beautiful, wrought iron buffet with a wooden top. I had to have it. In the middle of negotiating for it, I happened to see my neighbor at the sale, looking at a large, wooden trunk that the seller was offloading for a friend. We both ended up negotiating. I paid for the buffet, and the seller offered to deliver it to me. He called later to say when he was coming by, and by the way, his friend wanted to know if my neighbor wanted the trunk. I ended up negotiating for her, and he delivered both pieces for free.

You can also ask to pick up the item later. It would be an odd (and slightly stupid) seller who would lose a sale by refusing such a request, especially if you're clearly willing to buy. Arrange a convenient time and exchange phone numbers. If you're going to do this, however, you need to leave at least a partial payment. It would be an equally odd (and stupid) seller who would agree to a later pick-up without monetary assurance that you'll be back; otherwise you could change your mind, and the seller would have

Sliding into Home

A few years ago, while Denise and her family were visiting from New Jersey, we decided to go to the beach one day. Four of us piled into one car, four into another. Lou went one way, but I happened to turn down a street I don't usually take and coincidentally came upon a garage sale. Two young women were sitting at the curb on blue velvet wingback chairs. Even though Lou and I had promised to take a break from buying furniture, I wanted two wingbacks for my living room but knew they cost hundreds of dollars new. I pulled over and asked, "How much?" One of them said, "Thirty." I assumed that meant for each. Denise and I exchanged looks, and I thought, Lou will kill me if I buy another piece of furniture. And how would I get them home? She agreed to hold them for me, took twenty as a deposit, and then corrected me: thirty dollars for both chairs. Denise and I high-fived and spent the next half an hour trying desperately to figure out how to sneak them into the house. I arranged with a neighbor to store them for a while, but in the end I tearfully confessed to Lou that I'd broken our no-furniture promise. When he finally stopped laughing, he asked when we could go pick up the chairs.

lost an opportunity to sell the piece to someone else. And don't leave even a partial payment without getting a signed and dated receipt, but of course you didn't need me to tell you that. Sellers are honest people like you, and a deal is a deal, but a deal is a better deal when it's in writing.

In this chapter

Getting Started

Finding Garage
Sales

Estate and
Bulk Sales

Planning Your
Route

2

Mapping Out Your Day

How much planning you need to do depends a lot on where you live. When I'm garage saling in my own neighborhood, I don't spend any time planning because I can pass a dozen sales or signs just by driving down one main street. Since I know my neighborhood, I don't bother with a map. But if I drive out to some other part of the city, then out come the maps, and I go through the steps I describe in this chapter.

Getting Started

I have to admit that after twenty years of garage saling, it's easy for me to say that first-timers have no reason to feel scared or intimidated. Think of it this way: garage sales, especially multifamily sales, can be like small block parties. People are friendly and glad to see you, even if you don't buy anything.

Still, it can feel weird or scary the first time, especially if you're out there with a purpose, shopping for something in particular and feeling a sense of high expectations or pressure to find it your first day. You may feel self-conscious digging through other people's stuff, or you don't know how to approach them, or maybe there's a bunch of people jostling to look at the same table you want to look at. Maybe you still think that all you'll find is junk.

Well, I'm here to tell you: that's all in your head. If you think about it, garage sales are not even as bad as department stores — which you visit all the time — because there you're dealing with commissioned salespeople showing you high-priced items and often subtly pressuring you to buy. There's no pressure at garage sales. Garage sales have personal stories behind them that you'll learn if you just open up and get to know people: this young woman is moving back home to be with her family, that older couple has a sale every spring and fall that the neighbors all look forward to. While it won't replace your social life (hopefully), garage saling can be an enjoyable social activity in a way that retail shopping is not.

The best thing to do if you feel insecure is to go with someone who's gone garage saling before. If you're walking down the street and happen to pass a garage sale, check it out instead of passing by. If there's a sale down the block or around the corner, walk to it. It's easy to leave if you don't like it, and home is close if you need to ask the sellers to hold something while you run back to get more money or your car.

Finding Garage Sales

I've said before — and not for the last time — that garage saling involves large amounts of serendipity. But if you have a goal in mind, like furnishing a new apartment or replacing your old and broken appliances, then whatever your experience level, you will benefit greatly from planning your shopping trips. This isn't like driving to the mall, where you know what merchandise each store carries.

Where do you find garage sales? Isn't it enough just to follow those hand-lettered signs tacked onto telephone poles in your neighborhood?

It's enough for a while, until you get tired of driving around the same streets every weekend. True, the sales will be different homes each time, but eventually you'll start to feel like you're seeing the same merchandise again and again. And maybe you don't live in a spread-out neighborhood like mine but in a dense urban area of multi-unit flats or apartments or in a revitalized industrial area and don't have lots of garage sales to choose from; you'll need to drive elsewhere in any case.

The first place many people look for things these days is the Internet, where finding garage sales is easy, though not always useful. A number of garage sale websites have classified ad boards with listings. The catch is that even though you can find these ads anywhere in the country (or the world, for that matter), the sites usually list sales only for one local area. One good site has lots of listings... for Oklahoma City.

Much more useful than garage sale websites are the classified ad sections of your local newspapers, which specialize in your area. Many of these have websites too, probably with their classifieds online, searchable by category or keyword. The daily paper may put garage sale listings together in a separate box that runs Thursday through Sunday, since virtually all sales take place on the weekend. They're probably listed under "garage sales" or "garage and moving sales," but it could be "yard sales." Smaller local or community papers will list garage sales as well. They don't always come out daily — maybe only one to three times a week — but they depend on advertising from a smaller readership area, so the sales they list should be located closer together. That's important when you're mapping out your shopping trips by location. Another good source of local listings are the free "pennysaver" classified ad papers you can usually find in the wire racks at the front of your supermarket.

Newspapers also list flea markets and swap meets, which you can think of as dozens or hundreds of garage sales in one place. In many cities they take place at a regular time and location, often a school or the parking lot of a drive-in movie theater. These may be listed separately in a boxed display ad. In addition to your local newspapers, you may find such large events advertised in specialized newspapers for antique shoppers and traders.

They may also be listed on your city's or county's official website, since these sites tend to focus on community services and often have something like a "things to do around town" section, a link to the chamber of commerce, a local business directory, or a community events calendar.

Enlightened local governments sometimes get into the act themselves, realizing that making yard sales into municipal events is a public service that boosts a sense of community. Venice, where we used to live, a fairly small city with a lot of outdoor life, holds meetings for residents to plan citywide yard sale days. Participating neighborhoods produce their own maps with the sales marked by stars and addresses; you can pick them up at local businesses. The city of San Leandro, near San Francisco, holds yard sale days in each of its five city council districts as part of its Neighborhood Cleanup Events, which include community picnics where residents can learn about city recycling programs and services for keeping their neighborhood clean and green. One recent yard sale day

Tip!

Don't overlook non-traditional sources of garage sale listings: your church or temple newsletter; the employee newsletter where you work; and community bulletins boards at local markets, co-ops, community centers, coffee houses, and other small businesses. By the same token, these are good locations to place ads for your own garage sales.

had more than one hundred families participate. Call your city council member and ask if your city or district has events like this.

Estate and Bulk Sales

Since you're looking through the classified ads anyway, it could be worth your while to scan the public notices section. Public notices are notices required by law to be published in newspapers of general circulation for the city or county where a particular action is taking place. Fictitious business name statements are the most typical example of public notices. Public hearing announcements and government bidding opportunities are common too.

Tip!

If you live near a college or university, you might find little sidewalk sales in the neighborhood of the dormitories or fraternity/sorority row, especially in late spring, when the out-of-town students unload all the books, posters, and other knick-knacks they don't want to pay to store or haul back home for the summer.

What you're looking for, however, are notices of estate sales and public bulk sales of personal property. In an estate sale, someone has died and his or her belongings are being sold off. Bulk sales usually involve unclaimed property — possibly possessions left for years in public storage, after the storage facility is unable to contact the original owner — or property sold to pay liens or creditors. Terms are usually cash only. The notice and conduct of these sales is sometimes regulated by law, but you don't need to be concerned about that, because the laws apply to the sellers, not the buyers. These sales could be advertised among the regular classifieds, but they're often under public notices because they're more likely to be seen by people with a genuine interest.

You've figured out by now that these are places you could possibly pick up some good deals. With bulk sales, the seller is auctioning things off, trying to raise whatever money can be raised, so you might get good prices if there are not many bidders. It's not uncommon for buyers to walk away with hoards of furniture and other stuff for a few dollars.

Estate sales may be auctions too, or prices may have been determined by professional appraisers, especially where antiques, artworks, or other valuables are for sale, or where the appraiser was hired because bereaved and emotional family members couldn't agree on prices. In other words, the seller, who may be a sale administrator and not a family member, may have little or no flexibility to bargain. That's not always the case, however, so you never know what you might find. Sometimes the survivors think everything grandma owned was an antique and want a small fortune for it; other times they can't wait to get rid of "all this old junk" at any price and don't know or care that some of it could be valuable. Estate sales can last for several days, so you can easily add them to your itinerary when mapping out your weekend.

Planning Your Route

To reduce and regulate traffic, Orange County permits countywide yard sale days four times a year and will fine you for holding one on other days. That's only an hour's drive away for me, so I can only hit that area every few months, but I know I can visit dozens of sales each time. With proper planning, of course. Orange County is a huge suburban sprawl, and I could easily waste all day driving around. But I don't, because I map out my garage saling route.

There are two basic ways to do this: by location and by time. They're different but interrelated. Mapping by location is useful if you'll be garage saling most of the day or in another part of town. Mapping by time is more useful if you have family commitments or some schedule to keep, and need to squeeze in as many sales as you can into a limited period.

1. **Location.** When you're planning a garage saling day by location, take a street map in one hand and a list of all the sales you plan to visit in the other (see sidebar "How to Map Your Route"). Then work down the list and mark the locations on the map. Finally, map a route that starts with the farthest sale from your home and moves in along the shortest or easiest routes, depending on your local traffic. In addition to saving gas and time, this method has the advantage of giving you a psychological boost as the day progresses: as your energy

starts to drag, you'll find your-self getting closer to home, not farther away.

2. **Time**. Map your route in basi-cally the same way, but order your stops based on starting and ending times instead of dis-tance. Most garage sales start fairly early, like nine in the morning, but many start at eight or even seven o'clock. Others don't start until ten. Ending times vary too, but somewhere between three and five in the afternoon is typical. If a sale half a mile from you starts at seven and one that's

Tip!

If there's one available for your area, get a laminated plastic map instead of a paper map. Laminated maps are easier to open up and fold over in the car and won't get worn or torn at the folds with handling. In addition, you can use sticky notes or ad-hesive dot labels on them to mark the sales, because they re-move easily without ruining the surface.

ten miles away starts at nine, then starting with the more distant one (mapping by location) means you won't reach the closer one until at least ten. That's three hours of prime shopping time you've lost. If you go the other direction, you could hit both sales as they open and still maybe hit another sale on the way or have time for a third stop before lunch, without rushing. That's mapping by time.

Don't try to hit every sale early though. Save some for the afternoon, if you can, especially on Sunday. Sellers get tired after two days of a busy sale and want to get rid of whatever they can, which means they start cutting prices and become much more willing to bargain. Church and charity sales in particular often post price reductions for their final hours; there might not be much left by then, but you can get it for a song (or a hymn).

Tip!

Get a map that has little icons for churches and schools. Churches often hold rummage sales, and flea markets often set up at high schools because there's so much space and usually no charge for holding them. A map with churches and schools marked can help you zero in on the locations, saving you some planning and driving time.

Whichever method you use, it's important to note which day or days each sale takes place. Some run only Saturday or only Sunday, some both days. You don't want to do all this planning and then show up on the wrong day. Now and then you can find sales on weekdays. Depending on your family or other commitments, you might want to split your garage saling over both days of the weekend and do half as much each day. Figure that if a sale lasts two days, there's probably a lot of stuff, so you don't have to rush to be there when it opens Saturday morning.

Another thing: be considerate. Showing up when a sale opens is fine and even expected, but some sellers will consider it an inconvenience at best and an invasion of privacy at worst if you arrive while they're still setting up and ask to start looking around. Others won't mind. Think of a sale's posted hours as business hours, during which regular people like you are giving up their privacy. Think

How to Map Your Route

In many places, garage sales are widely scattered, and you may have to drive to another town, or from town to town, to get to them. This is where mapping by location can be a big help.

1. Plan out your whole weekend on Thursday or Friday night. Gather together and sit down with all the local publications and classified sections we discussed at the beginning — your daily newspaper, the pennysavers, your church newsletter — and lay out the garage sale sections in front of you.

   You can also search for "garage sales" in the classifieds section of your newspaper's website. These let you search by date, so you can generate separate garage sale lists for each day, which you can then print. However you do it, once your listings are in hand, start by circling all the ads that are either in your area or seem to have what you want.

2. Get out your map of the area (and your magnifying glass — see chapter 3), and mark in pencil the locations of all the addresses in the ads. Or use sticky notes or adhesive dots if you have a laminated map. That way you can plan your shopping route visually because you'll see where the sales are and which roads connect them. Once you figure out a route that makes sense, number the sales (on the map or stickies) in the order you're going to visit them.

3. Finally, make a list of the sales in the order you just mapped out. You can write the list by hand or cut out the ads and tape them in order onto some notebook paper. Then add notes and driving directions to the side if you want. Put it on a clipboard.

When you're finished, you'll have a numbered map and a matching detailed itinerary — with addresses, phone numbers, days, times, directions, and information about each sale — to use together as a working guide throughout the day or weekend.

about retail stores: You might want to be there when the doors open, but you wouldn't call the store manager at six in the morning to ask if he can open early for you.

Finally, every once in a while it's fun to try something new. Drive to a neighborhood you don't usually visit or even another part of town or another city that's nearby. Before long you'll get to know which neighborhoods have better prices or certain kinds of items. Plan the trip like I've described above, or just drive around if you're feeling adventurous or not in a hurry. Trust to serendipity.

However you do it, investing an hour to map out your shopping journeys will save you many hours and headaches once you're out there.

In this chapter

Your Basic Tool:
the Bag

In the Bag

3

Tools of the Trade

I can't even tell you how many times I've been out and wished I had some bubble wrap with me. I don't usually carry my supplies if I'm not planning to go out garage saling. So if I'm walking down the street and happen to pop into a thrift shop, naturally they have exactly the china bowl I've been trying to find for months, and I don't have any bubble wrap. Nine times in ten they'll wrap it in newspaper for me, but bubble wrap protects fragile things better. If I had some in my car, I'd run out to get it.

There have also been times when I was doing a lot of shopping and just dumped everything in my trunk, wishing I had a bag to keep it all concealed in. I ended up using my trunk to stash small jewelry and glassware, which is not a great idea if you want to find it again, much less find it in one piece. Other times I've run out of change. Or I haven't had my magnifying glass with me. If I had a bag, I used to think, I could keep all my supplies and all or most of my purchases in one place.

Finally, I got tired of wishing for someone to make the perfect garage saling bag, so I designed my own — a bag that does what a garage sale gourmet needs it to do. (Quick plug: You can find ordering information in Appendix B.) Now when I unexpectedly need change for a meter or a magnifying glass to inspect a piece of porcelain — or a safe place to stash my purchases — I have a place for all of it.

If you're going to be serious about garage saling — and I don't mean just addicts like me and my sister-in-law — you should have a garage saling bag. You will especially appreciate it at flea markets when you have to carry your purchases around because it's a pain to keep running back to your car to stash them away. And when you do keep returning to your car between garage sales, you'll have a convenient way to carry things back. Also, you won't have to hassle with grabbing up a bunch of scattered change and equipment every time you get out of the car, because you'll have it all in one place.

Your Basic Tool: the Bag

Let's talk about what makes an ideal garage saling bag. The main thing is to get a good, sturdy carrying bag. Any heavy-duty canvas bag is fine, and it doesn't have to be too heavy; a cottony canvas bag will hold up well too.

As important as the bag material are the handles, especially if you plan to carry the bag around all day. If you prefer to carry it on your shoulder, then believe me, you really want a flat leather or woven strap, because a round, ropy one will cut into your shoulders. A ropy handle is easier and more comfortable to carry by hand, however. My GSG bag has both handles, so your fingers and shoulders can give each other a break at any time.

You also want the bag to be roomy. I could have put that small chandelier I bought into a properly sized bag. A duffel bag with a zippered opening along the top is good. It's big but not too deep, so you can stash long objects in it but things don't get lost at the bottom. You don't want one with the opening at an end, because you'll have to reach all the way in to get anything. Also, I prefer zippers over snaps, which tend to pop open and let everything fall out. Actually, only the easily breakable items will fall out, if you know what I mean.

Finally, you want a bag with pockets so you don't have to keep your equipment, especially little items, in the main compartment, where you'll have a hard time finding it underneath your purchases. The GSG bag has a pocket for this book as well as outside and inside pockets for change, keys, pen, notebook, water bottle, or anything else you need to reach easily or just don't want to lose.

In the Bag

Most of the supplies you want to carry are simple things you probably have around the house or can buy inexpensively if you don't. Between your local drugstore, hardware store, and moving supplies store, you should have no problem finding everything.

I've compiled this list after finding these things useful in a pinch or wishing I had them. They're broken down into three categories: supplies you'll want to have handy in the car, what you'll need at the sales, and what you'll need to wrap things to take home. You may not need everything, so just carry what you do need. Probably the heaviest thing on the list is the camera, so it's not like you'll be carrying around tons of equipment. That's the last thing you want. Besides, much of it you can leave in the car until you've bought something and are ready to haul it away. There's a checklist of these items in Appendix B for easy reference.

Car Supplies
Here are a few things you'll want to have handy in the car.

- **Food**. Bring snacks and plenty of water. A day or morning of driving and walking can make you hungry, and you might or might not pass any place to stop for a snack. If you're a mom and dragging kids around, you don't need me to explain. But whoever you are, you'll want to keep your energy up.

- **Maps**. Any Thomas Guide or foldable city map will do. Maps are good to keep in the car anyway, and when you're out for a day of garage saling, especially with kids, you don't want to waste time driving around half lost. Laminated maps have several advantages that I mentioned in the last chapter, but here they are again: They're smaller than paper maps and fold more easily, so you can whip them out and put them back without fumbling. They don't get crumpled or torn. And you can stick colored labels or sticky notes on them to mark your route and destinations, then peel them off.

- **Weather clothing**. Depends on your local weather. All I'm saying is, you never know. I'm a Virgo, so I always overpack, but I've shopped with Denise in hailstorms and slush and sleet as well as 120-degree heat.

Field Supplies

These are the items you'll want to carry as part of your regular kit. You'll especially need them at places like flea markets, where you'll have a large selection and may want to compare the wares of different sellers. These items are also handy if you've got your room lists (from the first chapter) and are looking for something specific.

- **Tape measure.** It's amazing how many times I've gone to a thrift shop and the salesperson had to dig around or ask someone else to find a tape measure.

Your ruler doesn't have to be long or fancy — about the only thing you'll find at a sale that's more than six feet tall or wide is an armoire or sofa — and the inches on those little freebie tape measure key chains are the same inches you'll find on a $50 professional carpenter's model. Besides, a keychain tape measure can double as, duh, a keychain, where you can keep a spare key to the trunk of your car for quick loading. The main drawbacks with the freebies is that they aren't very durable and they aren't very long. Six feet may be fine for measuring small tables and chairs, but a ten-footer gives you enough length to measure spaces. I say spring the few bucks at your local hardware store and get a good tape measure that you can stretch across a living room.

- **Magnifying glass**. This is good for at least two things. Reading maps is one. The other is reading the tiny markings on porcelain, silver, china, and jewelry. Jewelry is sometimes signed, but the script can be hard to see. Same with the hallmark on sterling silver. China and porcelain may be stamped, but on older pieces the stamp could be mostly rubbed off or faint from wear. If you're collecting jewelry, you may want to get a jeweler's loupe.

- **Flashlight**. A flashlight is useful for getting a good look underneath sofas or inside cabinets to see wear and tear, cracks in the wood, or chipping of the finish.

You can also use it to look through things. Hold a flashlight up behind a piece of clothing, for instance, and you'll see like an X-ray where the fabric is worn by how brightly the light shines through.

- **Black light.** If you buy a lot of ceramics or porcelain, a pocket-sized black light is a good investment. It highlights cracks or chips that are hard to see in natural light as well as the thin white lines of glue that show where a piece has been repaired, which a flashlight won't reveal. You especially want to know this about old, rare, or potentially valuable pieces.

- **Batteries or extension cord.** You'll need these if you're planning to buy electronics or electrical tools or appliances. Most sellers won't have them readily available. Four AA and four C batteries should power up most toys, games, or radios. An extension cord or power strip may help for running a line from inside a seller's home to the yard. Carry the batteries; leave the extension cord in the car until you need it.

- **Pen and paper.** For taking notes, writing down measurements, and updating your shopping lists. If you prefer to use pencil, use a mechanical one (with extra leads stashed in the barrel) so you don't have to carry a sharpener.

- **Coin purse**. You probably have one in your purse or wallet already, but keep an extra one in your bag, stocked with quarters and dimes for parking meters. You also want to have plenty of small change when you're negotiating, so keep a few dollars in singles as well.

- **Camera**. Ten years ago I would've said get a Polaroid, but today it's all about digital. Digital cameras are great for comparing two similar items, say, on opposite sides of a flea market. Take a shot of each one and flip between them in the viewer. But there are more versatile options than cameras, namely cell phones and PDAs. Many models now come with built-in cameras and wireless Internet ability, so you can take pictures and send them digitally as well.

- **Cell phone or PDA**. A cell phone is great if you're shopping for friends, because if you run across something one of them wants, you can take a picture of it, send it to your friend's phone, then call and negotiate over the phone if the friend likes what she sees. A PDA may be better if you carry around reference photos of rooms or furniture pieces, like we discussed in chapter 1; the larger screen will give you a bigger, sharper image. In addition, PDAs usually come with word processing and spreadsheet applications (you can get shopping list applications too), so you can keep your lists and photos conveniently together. To top it off, some PDAs have cell phones in them, so you have everything in once place.

- **Instant handle.** You know how your thumb and fingers sometimes can't reach the handles of a store bag if you put something wide in it? This handle solves that for about two dollars at most moving supplies stores. The handle is a wooden or plastic cylinder about four inches long and one-half or three-quarters of an inch in diameter, with a metal wire running through it that has hooks on both ends. You hook the hooks onto the thin handles of a shopping bag or a box you've tied up with string, and voila! — instant carrying case.

Tip!

In a pinch, you can use a dollar bill as a tape measure because U.S. currency is almost exactly six inches long, depending on how much it's shrunk with crinkling. Lay one bill along what you're measuring, mark the end with your thumb, then slide it down and measure again, inchworm-style. Fold it in half, or thirds, or half and then thirds, to get units of three, two, or one inches. In addition, a bill is almost exactly two and one-half inches wide.

- **Reference books.** These are not something to carry in the bag but to keep in the car. The best place to leave them may be at home, although you can find handbooks and pocket guides suitable for toting along. If you're looking for items of a particular style or period, like Depression glass, you'll want an authoritative reference and pricing guide that can show you what's available, what it's worth, and how you can spot reproductions or fakes.

Packing Supplies

Once you've bought things, especially large or fragile items, you'll need some way of securing them in your car for bringing them home. Keep these things in your trunk so they're there when you need them.

- **Scissors**. For cutting string, wrapping paper, bubble wrap, and so forth. If you stick the points into a cork, they won't stab or tear things.

- **Wrapping material**. Stash some newspaper or bubble wrap for dishes or glassware. You can buy bubble wrap with quarter-inch bubbles in handy little rolls. You can use Scotch tape to secure wrapping paper, but I prefer rubber bands because they're easier to store and carry (you can wear them like bracelets). They're better than tape for holding small boxes closed, and, unlike tape, they don't get hair and lint stuck to them, so you don't wind up with crumpled balls of hairy tape rolling around the floor of your backseat.

- **Boxes**. Carry some cardboard boxes if you expect to be buying and transporting glassware. Moving supplies stores often sell boxes with partitions specifically made for glassware. Keep them flat until you're ready to pack something. In that case, you might want to keep a roll of packing tape around too.

- **Packing tape.** For securing boxes, but it works for wrapping paper and bubble wrap as well.

- **Plastic bags**. Thirteen-gallon plastic garbage can liners are good for additional storage. Use them when you have to transfer your purchases out of your garage saling bag to leave them in the trunk.

- **Casters.** If you're shopping for large furniture items, then wheeled casters make it much easier to get them from a sale to your car, and from your car into your home.

- **Padding.** Transporting furniture can damage your purchases as well as your car's upholstery. You can buy specialized furniture padding at any moving supplies store, but old blankets and sheets work fine too.

- **Ropes, ties, and straps.** It will be well worth the money to invest in some flat straps with buckles for securing furniture pieces to a roof rack (or the roof, if you're desperate). A twenty-five-foot length of rope, nylon, or cotton cord is enough for most situations. Each material has advantages and disadvantages. Rope is strongest but has a scratchy texture, a difference your hands and furniture will notice. Cotton holds well, but a tight knot can be hard to untie. Nylon stretches the most, so furniture may shift and come loose, but it will serve for securing things in the bed of a pickup. Elastic bungee cords are adaptable to different situations and easy to stow, but they're short and you really have to watch out that the exposed hook ends don't gouge or scratch things. However, bungees are great for preventing your trunk lid from flapping when an end table fits — but not all the way.

Once you've got all your equipment together, leave your field supplies in the bag and packing supplies in the car so that everything's ready to go when you are. Food and maps — and your shopping lists and itinerary — you can gather when the weekend comes.

You're ready to hit the road.

In this chapter

4

Hitting the Streets

At last, we grab our lists, lock the house, toss our garage saling bags in the car, and start hitting the sales. Assume the position!

First, Remember These Three Things

1. People just want to get rid of their stuff. That's the single most important thing to keep in mind. Think about what you'd tell a little child who's afraid of a gopher popping its head up: He's more afraid of you than you are of him. Garage sellers are more afraid of you — that you won't buy anything and they'll have to haul the

whole load back into their garage or house — than you are of them. You can always walk away. They can't.

2. Just because someone is clearing out their house doesn't mean anything's wrong with their belongings. You're not getting ripped off. Often they're just selling unwanted gifts. Or the sellers bought something and then changed their minds, or never wore it when it was in style, or found something they liked better, more suited to their decor. Or they're moving and don't have room for it in their new apartment. Or they bought it at a garage sale too and ended up never using it. You can find all kinds of new and like-new things at garage sales.

3. Most things, including damaged ones, can be repaired, polished, or painted, and they look like new, or at least the way you want them to look. Something appeals to you but it's all covered in dust? Imagine it cleaned up and polished and on your bookshelf or dining table. Imagine weather-beaten furniture with a coat of paint or new cushions that match your living room. Use your imagination.

What You Can Learn in a Five-Second Drive-By

You're in your car and approaching a garage sale that's not on your plan. You just saw the sign on a telephone pole, so there's no ad or note on your itinerary that this sale has anything for you. You slow down to five miles an hour and keep one eye on your driving as you cast the other across the garage sale scene, scoping it out. You'd probably do this anyway, without even thinking. But if you think about it, you can be more effective. A few simple signs can give you a better idea of whether a yard sale is likely to have what you want.

The first thing to notice is what's placed at the curb. This is what sellers want you to notice. It's the lure, usually at least one big ticket item, like some nice furniture — perhaps a set, a dining table and chairs, placed near the curb or slightly away from other things. When it sells, out comes the next big item — so this can give you a clue to what else is for sale. Featuring it means the seller really wants to get rid of it, so you can often get a good deal.

Second, notice how many items are for sale. Not a number, obviously, just a sense of how big the sale is. Maybe it's not big, so is it worth your time? It could be, if you spot at least one thing that catches your eye. If it's a big sale, start looking for parking.

Finally, take a look at who's doing the selling. An elderly woman likely has jewelry for sale, and chances are good that not all of it will be out on the tables. Ask if she's selling more than what's displayed. A man may have electronics and sporting goods. Someone college-aged is possibly moving and may have books and lots of small home furnishings. Looking at the sellers won't always reveal anything, but it might be a reason to visit.

That's all you have time for. Want to stop? If nothing strikes you in a five-second drive-by, forget it. There are greener pastures to graze.

Second First Impressions

Once you've gotten out of the car, collect your first impressions of the sale up close. Is this the kind of sale where you'll want to shop? Are there a lot of people shopping? Notice how everything is displayed. If it's planned and neat, you're probably dealing with experienced sellers who know their prices and who have learned to give some thought to their visitors' shopping experience. Notice if the sale area on the lawn or in the garage is clean and safe and whether the sellers are paying attention to their customers or busy visiting with each other, watching TV, or eating lunch. Whether they say hello when you arrive or even acknowledge you until you hand over something to buy it. Listen to how they negotiate with other customers.

Looking around a garage sale doesn't take much instruction. Pass what doesn't interest you and look at what does, and keep in mind the third of the three points we discussed at the beginning: Use your imagination. But also note prices. As you visit more and more sales, you'll develop a sense of reasonable pricing, especially for

Tip!

Shop for seasonal items one season early, like ice chests in spring and umbrellas in summer. Once the season hits, everyone will want them and prices will go up.

household items like appliances that you come across frequently. Some sellers price things low because they're afraid people won't buy, while others believe everything they're selling is valuable, so they price it all too high. Conventional wisdom is that buyers will pay about one-third to one-half the retail price for items in good condition. You'll get familiar with prices — and learn to bargain more effectively — with time and experience.

Notice if a seller has a lot of any particular kind of item, like toys, tools, sporting goods, or furniture. The first three could simply indicate that there's a guy in the house, but any of them could mean that the seller went looking for them cheaply and in quantity, probably on clearance racks and from other garage sales, for the purpose of reselling them at a profit. The display may resemble a clearance rack itself. So here's someone you know has already jacked up the prices. Or maybe not; sometimes people just have a lot of something. Either way, it's an opportunity to bargain by offering to take several items for one price slightly lower than their combined individual prices. And there may be a good selection.

See if there's anything for sale that's on your shopping lists. That's why we're here, remember? Get out your lists, your magazine cuttings, your digital photos. If you find a possible match, you've got a measuring tape and magnifier in the garage saling bag on your shoulder.

If you find a sale that has great prices and a lot of things you need, don't be in a hurry to get to the next sale on your itinerary. Finding a great sale is one of the biggest pleasures of garage saling, so shop it out thoroughly before you leave. Some days you hit a lot of small, uninteresting sales, and you'll wish you'd stayed longer at the good ones. If nothing excites you, you'll know quickly. Scratch that sale off your itinerary, get in the car, and move on.

Tip!

If you like an item but can't decide whether to buy it, pick it up anyway and carry it around. You can always put it back, but if you don't pick it up, you can be sure someone else will — at the exact moment you decide you want it.

Negotiating Know-How

You don't need the skills of a hostage negotiator to bargain at a yard sale. What's to be afraid of? You've got the advantage. People hold yard sales because they want to get rid of things. That was the first key point to remember — remember? What they don't sell they're either going to drag back into the garage, donate, or haul out with the trash. On balance, it's worth sacrificing a few bucks to avoid any of that work. People often don't know how much to sell things for and will take a reasonable offer. What's the right price for something you don't want anyway? As a garage sale shopper, if you don't ask for a better price, you won't get one. Ask, and you probably will. Make an offer.

Basically, you want to live by these three principles:
1. Know how much you want to pay for something.
2. Be firm about how much you're willing to pay.
3. Be willing to walk away.

Here are some tips for negotiating better deals.

- **Carry mostly small denominations.** You'll be able to pay with closer to exact change, so you'll feel like you have more flexibility in bargaining. Negotiating for a lower price is expected, but being a cheapskate is tacky and bad karma too. For example, don't bargain someone from $30 down to $5 and then hand them a $50 bill. If you only want to pay ten dollars for an item that's selling for fifteen, take out two fives and say this is all you have. In most cases, when a seller sees green, he or she won't say no. They'd rather take a few dollars less than they'd hoped for than nothing at all.

Tip!

Check underneath price labels to see if the seller is slyly covering up chips or scratches, especially on china and polished surfaces. Cover-ups are not cool, but some people do it anyway.

- **Come back later**. If a seller is firm on price but you don't want to pay it, come back at the end of the day or the next day. If it's not there, it wasn't meant for you anyway. If it is, the seller may be willing to come down in price rather than blow another opportunity with the sale nearing its end. A couple hours before closing time is when sellers become more willing to drop prices. In fact, that's when many bargain hunters are out in force.

- **Buy more than one item**. You can often get a better price if you buy more than one thing. This is easy if you're with friends, because you can pool your selections. Your shopping list can help here, if a sale has several items on the list. Tell the seller, "I'm (or we're) going to take all of this. Can you give me one good price?" Suggest one that's less than the combined prices. Chances are that even for less money, a seller will consider it a good deal just to be rid of several things at once.

> **Tip!**
>
> Ask yourself whether you're negotiating for something you actually need or merely want. If you need it, then take everything into account, not just price. Will it fit the room? Is it the right style? Does it fit into my total budget? If it really is all those things, paying a little more may still prove a bargain.

- **Communicate clearly**. When you pool purchases, be clear about what you're proposing to buy. Sellers will give a better price if they think you're taking more than one thing, but if you negotiate a price and then don't take some of it, or want to add an item, they'll justifiably get annoyed.

- **Make exceptions**. Know how much you want to spend, but if a seller is not willing to bring down a higher price for something you really want or need, be willing to stretch your own limit if you know you're going to regret not buying it. This is the exception, not the rule. If you don't buy it, you may curse yourself — but only until you find something the following week you like better, for less money.

If you see something you just want, regardless of the outcome of negotiations, then rationality won't be much help. "It really caught my eye," you'll say to justify it in your mind. "I don't really need it, but it's so unusual..." Maybe you had no intention of buying it, maybe it even costs a lot. But then you start thinking automatically about where it will go in the house, where you'll wear it. I once bought myself a necklace and earring set this way. I wasn't looking for one, but the price was right. I would have spent that much on lunch without even thinking about it. Now I get compliments whenever I wear it.

Tip!

Keep your money in your pocket, a coin purse, or even a fanny pack. You won't have to fumble around for loose change, and a fanny pack is more convenient than a purse, which can knock breakable things over when you carry it and get stolen when you don't. On the other hand, if you rummage around in your pocket or fanny pack long and unsuccessfully enough, looking for those last few cents, you might get lucky and the seller will say forget about it.

Household Stuff

You won't be buying just decorative items for your home. Garage sales are great for finding household and personal items. They may not be on any of your lists, but you need them anyway, utilitarian items like toasters or drinking glasses. Maybe more so than clothing, household items are the most common merchandise out there: silverware, bookends, place settings, lamps, hair brushes, coffee makers, and so forth. If you can think of it, you can probably find it.

Clothing is a mixed proposition. Designing a good wardrobe usually means building it around looks and outfits, not individual pieces, which makes garage sales an unpromising venue for conventional wardrobe building. On the other hand, they are great for creating an eclectic, mix-and-match wardrobe for very little money, since adult clothing is not a big seller and you can get good prices. If clothing is your thing, however, and building an eclectic wardrobe is your main goal, you'll have more consistent luck at thrift and vintage clothing shops, where the selections are much greater and the turnover of items is high.

Garage sales are better for finding disposable clothing or work clothing. By disposable, I mean children's clothing, just because they outgrow it so fast. Regardless of how disposable or rugged, you should expect all clothing to be in decent condition and at least washed for display. Pass on items that have anything more than light stains anywhere, especially under the arms. Stains that haven't come out yet aren't coming out for you either. If an item smells stale or like mothballs from storage, a good airing might fix that, or it might not. If it smells of the last person who wore it, forget about it. This kind of embarrassment you don't need, no matter how cheap the item. And shame on the seller for putting it out.

Garage sales are good places to buy accessories and costume jewelry too, sometimes even authentic pieces, either by design or because a hapless seller couldn't tell pearls from beads. Belts, purses, and shoes are other good bets.

Especially when buying kids' clothing, don't rely on tag sizes, because the clothes will have been washed many times and shrunk. Instead, bring one of your kid's shirts or pants or dresses to use as a size guide. The pitfall here is that the seller may think you're buying both the items you're comparing. If you want to do this, show the seller the items you're bringing, so there won't be any argument over them later.

You'll find lots of things for kids, besides clothing, such as strollers, toys, playpens, high chairs, and changing tables. The toy sections, especially at church sales, can be fun for toddlers to play in while you look around, and your kids can preview a number of toys before you let them pick one. Look also for toys that are bagged together for one price. On the other hand, you don't want to buy toys or high chairs — or anything — with broken or missing pieces, no matter how inexpensive. Simple problems like a broken crib slat or a toy trunk lid that doesn't prop up can pose serious dangers.

Other things I wouldn't recommend buying, no matter what the bargain, include expired over-the-counter drugs, or prescription drugs of any age, or mascara, which can easily become contaminated — not something you'd want near your eyes. I once found a Mary Kay samples case full of discontinued items; it was never opened, so it might have been okay, but I wouldn't have chanced it. I didn't need it anyway. Never buy chemicals, hazardous or not, because how can you really be sure what's in an open bottle? Halloween costumes that aren't flame resistant are out too, though I can't imagine there are many more of those still around. Also out are old hair dryers and electrical cords or appliances without safety certification labels.

Tip!

Take off price tags as soon as you get home. The longer a sticker stays on, the harder it usually is to remove, and the more adhesive gunk stays behind.

In general, you can follow the same approach with household items as you would with home furnishings: If it doesn't work out, you've only lost a few dollars. But most things work out fine.

Thinking Positive

Be optimistic. Success comes in waves. Some days I find Snoopy collectibles everywhere, or lamps and desks at every sale, and some days I come home in the afternoon with nothing. Don't expect to find everything you want at the first sale or even on the first day. Your neighbors won't always be ridding themselves of exactly what you need. On the other hand, I once bought an outdoor, iron candle holder for four dollars when I wasn't even looking for one, and now it's one of my favorite pieces for the patio.

Then there are days like my daughter Chloe's birthday party. The day before, I'd stopped at an apartment garage sale, and the woman held my purchases for me while I ran to the ATM. Later I snuck it all into the house. On party day I went out with my sister-in-law

Denise to get ice. As usual, we had ulterior motives. We passed a yard sale sign, and I noticed it had the same address as the previous day. However, this particular sign looked different, and far be it from us to miss a sale. In fact it was the same location, but a different seller who lived in the same complex, and she had lots of stuff out. I parked the car and couldn't shop quickly enough. I grabbed the items that caught my eye as if hordes of customers were pushing and shoving to buy the same items. After several minutes of this, our new best friend totaled my finds, and naturally I had no cash, just a debit card. She offered to hold my items while I went to the ATM, which happened to be in the market where, oh yeah, I was getting ice for a party of sixty guests who would be arriving at any minute.

We got back to the sale in record time, loaded my trunk, and returned to my house and a back yard full of guests. One by one, Denise and I snuck my new purchases into the house and strategically placed them as if they had been

there all along, thinking Lou would-
n't notice, at least not right away. It's
funny how observant he became that
day, though he was not surprised at
my ability to shop at a garage sale
while getting ready to throw a party.
Over time he has accepted the fact
that I sometimes bring my garage sale
purchases into our house unan-
nounced. And he eventually had to
confess that he liked what I bought.

Tip!

You can fit more
clothes into a bag if
you roll the items up
like sausages instead of
stuffing them in. Re-
member that if you're
at a sale with a "fill a
bag for $5" offer.

Days like my big score don't happen often enough, but
they do, and you'll never know when. If you want to put
some method into your shopping madness, work your
weekend plans but leave lots of room for chance. You're
not spending a lot of money, so it's cheap to experiment
with new things. You may find the table that's the missing puzzle piece in the home you picture for yourself, or
something you stumble across could become the corner-
stone for that room where you were drawing a blank.

Be open to what the world and your neighbors'
garages have to offer. Learn to look past the dirt and
chipped paint and visualize the things on someone else's
lawn inside of your home — reupholstered, repainted,
ready for their new life.

Part Two
Home Cookin'

In this chapter

When and Why to Research Things

Shopping Research

Hitting the Books

5

So, What Did You Get?

Whether you're collecting fine Wedgwood or crystal pieces or just buying an armoire for your daughter's growing wardrobe, paying garage sale prices instead of retail for collectibles or big ticket items will give you quite a psychological boost. Better yet is the sense of accomplishment at the end of the month when you find extra money in your checking account.

You increase the money you save at garage sales when you understand how much you can and should spend, and the way to do that is through some simple research. I don't mean trips to the library, but if you get serious about collecting antiques or other collectibles, you may do that too. Our focus here is on the simple kinds of research you can do that will enable you to take the home inventory you've created and find out what it's all worth, or at least what it should all cost, new and used.

When and Why to Research Things

Once you know a range of prices, you have more information to help you decide what you're willing to pay. Think of your research as comparison shopping.

You can do research either before or after you buy, but some things you'll definitely want to research before, and others it won't matter even after. If you're collecting, you'll want to study the pricing guides before you shop and consult them with your purchases in hand later. If you suspect that a piece of costume jewelry you bought might actually be the real deal, you can take it to a jeweler for appraisal. That's research too. Furniture may be more difficult to appraise. Sometimes your research is accidental. Remember the chair I bought that nearly ripped up my car? I didn't know it was vintage until I tried to resell it. Everyone who sat in it to try it out told me it was old. Of course I acted like I already knew that, but I made sure to check it out later.

You should research furniture in advance, for price as well as style or period, because it can save you money to know this. On the other hand, if you merely want something nice to match your room, it doesn't matter if you research a furniture piece before or after. I once bought a dining table I liked, so it didn't matter if it was really mahogany underneath all the layers of paint, like the seller said. But I already knew what new and used dining tables cost, so when I paid for it, I felt that I got a good deal. When I got those two wing chairs for thirty dollars on the way to the beach, I knew just from shopping research that they would sell new for twenty times that amount.

Some things you should research before you buy, and it's a bad idea not to. Antiques spring to mind, but this book doesn't cover them because even though you might get lucky and find one, antiques comprise a complex and specialized market, and garage sales are not the best place to look. Collectibles, however, you might run across anywhere, and by researching them beforehand, you'll know what you're looking for and recognize a find when you see one. We'll discuss collectibles in the next chapter.

Finally, you should do research on anything you intend to buy for its value, whether you're keeping it or reselling it. You need to know what you can afford to pay and still make a profit.

Shopping Research

If you're buying things at garage sales to resell them, either at your own sale or on auction sites like eBay, then you need to know street values in order to know what you're doing. Let's look at some simple ways to educate yourself.

Retail Stores

Say you're looking for a coffee table. Start by visiting department and furniture stores to see what they cost new, particularly items that are similar in size and style to what you want. This will set your ceiling price, and seeing a lot of pieces will stimulate your imagination and prepare you to spot the one you want. Then look in thrift shops, shops with unfinished and refinished furniture (professional repair and refinishing will figure into the price), and your local Goodwill store. You might even find what you want inexpensively without looking any further. If not, you now have a range of prices. Keep notes on your findings attached to the coffee table item in your shopping list.

Retail Store Websites

If you can't get to the stores, bring the stores to you. Check out the websites of major retailers like Sears, Ikea, Montgomery Ward, Macy's, or any other store you know of that carries furniture, and see what kind of coffee tables they sell, and for how much. I wouldn't buy through the websites unless you really want to pay shipping and handling on large, heavy pieces. All you're looking at now are styles and prices.

Auctions

Visit eBay and other auction sites to see what other people are asking for coffee tables. One random day I found nearly five hundred coffee tables for sale, ranging in price from $20 to $2,000. That's not much help, but once I narrowed

down the search to a certain style, age, or other character-
istic, the range closed up to something with meaning.

Manufacturer
This works especially well for glassware and collectibles,
where items are often sought by the names of their makers, like Wedgwood or Candlewick. These companies have
websites too, which may include online auctions as well
as product guides.

Needless to say, there is so much shopping taking place on
the Internet that most or all of these methods can be useful
for researching furnishings of almost any type. Keep good
notes so that you get familiar not only with the prices you
can expect to see at garage sales (conventional wisdom says
one-third of retail price for items in good condition) but
also how factors like age and condition affect street price.

Hitting the Books

Think of something to collect and there's almost certainly
a book about collecting it. I'm talking about reference
books, which you will need if collecting is what you want
to do. However, I don't suggest lugging them around in
your garage saling bag. Many of them are coffee table
books, large and heavy, with lots of pictures so you can appreciate the beauty of fine china, jewelry, Coca Cola para-
phernalia, model trains, or whatever. If you really get into

collecting, you can research specific pieces in pricing guides, but you'll be absorbing knowledge all the time because you'll want to read about and see all the pieces you can.

You can spend a fair bit of money on reference books if you get serious about collecting, but when you're getting started you can avoid spending anything until you know what you want to collect by sitting down with a small, discreet notebook in the collectibles aisle of Borders or Barnes & Noble. There you will find shelves full of pricing and product guides, most with photos, for almost any type of collectible you can imagine and then some (see sidebar "Types of Collectibles" in the next chapter). Just don't look like you're conducting a major research project. You might want to take breaks to browse around so you don't attract attention by hanging out in the same aisle for two hours. Make small talk with the sales staff to find out when the shift changes, and do half your research before and half afterward so the same salespeople don't keep seeing you.

I'm not saying you shouldn't buy the books. I'm just saying take a little time to compare the books and get to know your tastes and subject matter before you buy any-

Tip!

Pocket-sized field guides are available for certain glassware and collectibles so that you can identify pieces at garage sales, flea markets, and antique shows. Don't flash them around at the sales though. It will flag you as a collector. Alert sellers may ask higher prices since they know you're looking. Flip through the book discreetly, or go to the car to consult it.

thing. I list some of the major publishers in "Going Further" at the end of this book. There may be several books on popular collectibles like Depression glass, and you probably don't need all of them. Spending time with them in the aisle will tell you which books and publishers you find most useful, as well as get you more familiar with the subject. Once in a Barnes & Noble I learned that a Candlewick china set I owned was the only set made in that style, and it turned out to be worth a fair amount of money. All it cost me to find this out was a few minutes of browsing. It doesn't have to cost you more.

In this chapter

6

Collecting Collectibles

A few years ago I was cleaning out my garage when I came across something I didn't know I still had: a little Snoopy bookend I bought at a department store when I was nine years old. I've always loved Snoopy, and I was really happy to find that I still had the piece after all these years. After I got the bookend, my mom bought me two books — *Happiness Is a Warm Puppy* and *We Love You, Snoopy* — at a now defunct department store called The Treasury. Since then I've bought Snoopy toys, books, statuettes, phones, and anything else I could find, whenever I could. Today I own more than three thousand Snoopy items, and my collection has been valued at thousands of dollars.

That's way more than I paid for it. Peanuts items are easy to find at garage sales, where you can pay dollars or cents for items with a much higher book value. That's true of many types of collectibles, some of which you might not realize are valuable. That means most sellers don't know either, making garage sales an excellent venue to bargain for collectibles.

Why Collect Anything?

It's hard to say exactly what it is about sets and collections that appeals to people. Collectibles often fall into certain established categories, like art glass or toys, but they also tend to have one or more particular qualities that make people connect with them emotionally. Perhaps they evoke nostalgia for a particular period, like the 1950s, or were part of a momentous or historical event, like a world's fair. Or they're associated with celebrities; there's a huge collectibles market in movie posters. Or they're obsolete, or made by a company with a long-standing reputation for quality, like Fabergé.

Because of this emotional connection, a collection says a lot about who you are, which makes it a good way to add a distinctly personal element to your living environment. You can collect for aesthetic or monetary reasons, or both, as is usually the case with antiques. Either way, collecting says something about your sense of beauty, value, and personal style.

You don't have to be a collector in any official sense or read any books in order to use collections as a way of adding style and splash to your home environment. But if you are serious about collecting, there are literally thousands of reference books, websites, and other guides available to help you learn, along with a huge community of enthusiasts. You can focus on one particular item or category or collect a wide range of things, from furniture to movie memorabilia to decorated glass. You might not know what to collect until something catches your eye. I'd never heard of Candlewick china until a woman I work with told me about it. She started talking about the pattern on a candy dish she had, and then she brought in a Candlewick picture book. I instantly fell in love with it. There's lots of information out there for Candlewick collectors; it's highly sought after, and people sell it because they know they can get a good price.

No matter how you do it, collecting starts with a passion for something, and our passions and tastes change as we go through life. That means any time is a good time to start. How about now?

Collections or Collectibles

The popularity of TV appraisal shows like *Antiques Roadshow* just goes to show how badly people want to believe they own something valuable. Sometimes they're right. You may have the start of a valuable collection at home;

you just don't know it yet. A collection often starts with just one piece, like my Snoopy bookend. At nine years old, I was not planning to start a collection that would become a lifelong passion or something I'd one day get appraised. I just thought Snoopy was cute.

The collectibles market is large and popular and written about in countless books, magazines, and websites for collectors of almost anything you could imagine collecting. The sidebar "Types of Collectibles" provides a list of categories for which I found price guides and picture books at just one bookstore on one day — which makes it a tiny list compared to the totality of what's out there. We're going to focus on the tactics you can use to find collectibles, and pay less for them when you do.

But collectibles are not all we're talking about here. Collections don't actually have to be of "collectible" items. The term *collectibles* is somewhat vague anyway, basically meaning anything people want to collect that isn't antique or more than one hundred years old. So you can collect whatever appeals to you, whether there's a book or category for it or not.

Maybe it's bowls. Yes, there are books about bowls, because famed glass makers like Candlewick made (and make) beautiful bowls that are now highly sought as collectibles. But how many bowls do you see every day in shops and malls and even at garage sales that aren't "collectible" but might look nice together if you just used your imagination? Use color to unify them. A shelf decorated with bowls of the same color but different styles and one

Types of Collectibles

Here are *some* of the kinds of items for which you can find books in the collectibles aisle of the bookstore:

- Avon perfume bottles
- Bakelite jewelry
- Bakelite kitchen utensils
- Barbie
- Baseball memorabilia (cards, posters, pennants, jerseys, team yearbooks)
- Bauer pottery
- Christmas ornaments
- Cigarette lighters
- Clocks and barometers
- Cobalt blue glass
- Coca Cola (bottles, glassware, ads, vending machines, etc.)
- Comic books
- Cups and saucers
- Depression glass
- Fabergé
- Fishing lures and tackle
- Football memorabilia (see Baseball)
- Handkerchiefs
- Hockey memorabilia (see Baseball)
- Hot Wheels and Matchbox cars
- Hummel figurines
- Jewelry
- Lionel trains
- Lunch boxes
- Marbles
- Mexican silver jewelry
- Military insignia
- Movie and celebrity memorabilia
- Musical toys
- Pez dispensers
- Political memorabilia
- Purses and handbags
- Quilts
- Radios
- Sewing tools and buttons
- Stamps
- Vinyl records
- Watches

with bowls of completely different patterns will create different but probably equally striking effects.

This is the kind of thing I'm talking about: collections, which could include collectibles. All we're doing is broadening the concept.

Do another inventory like the one we did in chapter 1, only this time with an eye toward collections or collectibles. Maybe you have candlesticks or lamps or flower vases scattered among different rooms that would make a powerful effect grouped together. Maybe you still have your old gold "leaf" glassware and Welch's grape jelly jar glasses with colorful Hanna Barbera cartoon figures from the 1960s and '70s. These are actually very popular collectibles that you can find at antique and collectibles shops. They're easy to find at garage sales too, and comparatively cheap. Why not take them out of your cupboard and display them to add a touch of fun to your home setting instead of hiding them in your cupboard? You can always buy a set at a garage sale to drink from.

Walk through your home with your inventory in hand, taking note of items you might have overlooked or not thought about previously. Maybe you have a decorative

Tip!

You don't actually have to be a collector to use the power of collections to enhance the look of your home. Once you have three of anything, they can look like a set if you arrange them like one. It hardly matters what they are. They can be similar items in different styles — like vases, teapots, or candlesticks — or different items of the same style or color, which will look like they go together.

old lamp that you suspect might be valuable, and that's what gave you the idea to start collecting. In that case, write it down, then get going like you keep telling yourself to do and find out what it's worth. Well, finish the inventory first. Maybe you have a carved or crystal bowl or other piece of fine or unusual glassware. There are more kinds of collectible glassware than you even realize.

Visit each room, including the kitchen and bathroom, and go through your shelves and drawers and cupboards with a sharp eye, preferably also with a beginner's guide to collecting, which will give you some specific ideas about what to look for. Items like lamps, porcelain figurines, and rock 'n' roll memorabilia might seem like obvious collectibles. Kitchen items like flatware, cookie jars, and toasters might not, but they often are. Just as you did with your original inventory, write down what you'd like to get for each room as well as what you have.

Here's where the last chapter's research work comes in. Once you've put together some notes — and hopefully the start of a collection or two — do research on what you have. Look over each piece you suspect may be collectible to see if there's a brand name or manufacturer (or artist's name, if it's unusual) imprinted on it, and then go down to your local chain bookstore and look for books about that category of item in the collectibles aisle. See whether people are selling similar items on eBay and how much buyers are bidding for them. You may not even realize you have a genuine collectible until you do this. Or you may not have one. At least you'll know.

Of course, you only need to do this if you're looking for collectibles. If you don't care about collectibles but just want a collection with visual flair, then go with what looks right to you. Remember, at garage sales you can experiment cheaply.

Buyer Beware

If I see a collectible I really want at a sale, I never act like I'm excited about it. That would be the worst thing to do. When a seller sees that you really, really want a piece, especially something collectible, the price may go up.

To avoid that, I'll pick a piece up and look it over, then pass it off like it's no big deal; then I come back to it later. I never tell people at their garage sales that I collect Candlewick or whatever. In fact, if a seller has some, I always pretend like it's for someone else. I've even trained my husband and kids to help out with this. Sometimes they even do it on their own, although once I got a little annoyed at Lou because he was making a big deal about not liking a $10 candelabra I'd looked at. "I'm just acting," he said, and I said, "Don't worry, she's already quoted a price."

Tip!

Because of their high value, antiques should be appraised and recorded for tax and insurance purposes, but that's not necessary for most collectibles, though some can be quite valuable or rare. There is a lot of literature surrounding antiques and their markets, and there is so much specialization that you're not likely to find genuine antiques at garage sales except by chance. You'll have a better shot at estate sales.

If the kids see something they know I like, they come up and tell me quietly instead of yelling across the yard, "Hey, Mom! Here's that Snoopy you've been looking for!" Or they'll call me a different name, anything but "Mom" or "Anita," as a kind of code. They're happy that they've helped me find something, and they have fun being little spies. Later, when people see the item in our home, the kids can point out with pride exactly who helped mom find it. And I got a good price because I didn't act desperate.

Tip!

Remember to tell your friends and family what you collect so they can be your eyes and ears.

The potential cost of repairs is important to consider when you're at the table, trying to decide whether to spring for that candelabra or not. Ask yourself if the cost of repairing a piece is going to exceed the price you pay for it at the sale, and by how much. Repairing a typical household item is not a big deal, but for collectibles and antiques, condition is more important than age in determining price.

Inspect wooden pieces for any trace of termite dust, which looks like a fine light powder. It's actually wood chewed up by little termite teeth. You might not see any dust if the piece has been wiped off, so get your magnifying glass out of your garage saling bag and look for signs of chewing — pinprick-sized termite holes, sometimes lots of them. You can tell which are termite holes by blowing a puff of breath into them, which will cause minute sawdust inside to puff back out. Then decide if you want to bargain the price down or pass.

Collecting Collectibles

Your magnifying glass will help you read the watermark on fine porcelain, the hallmark on fine silver, and the maker's stamp on some fine glassware, so you can learn something about a piece based on your reference books. Whip out your black light to look for fine cracks, chips, and the thin glue lines that show where a crack has been repaired. All these things will show up as bright white against the background of the finish, and they can lower an item's value significantly.

Be wary if a seller asks a high price for a piece because it's old or calls a crack a "hairline" or "age crack" to minimize its importance. That hairline crack will do more to reduce the value of the item than its age will to increase it. Sellers like this often think everything they have is collectible — rarely the case — or that everything old is valuable, so they price their items high. You'll get to recognize this. Other people don't know what they have, or don't care, and price everything cheaply. Collectors study items and prices and know what something is worth. A garage sale with a separate antiques or collectibles display means the seller clearly knows what he or she is selling, so you should plan to negotiate accordingly.

Does a piece show real artistic merit or skilled handwork, or is it a later production line knockoff? Does it bear the name of a designer, or is it unsigned and anonymous? Items that are name brands, signed, unique, or handmade can be worth much more than the mass-produced versions. For example, Art Deco items from the 1920s are singular pieces, often handcrafted from silver, ivory, fine woods, and

Garage Sale Gourmet

other exotic materials. But as new materials and manufacturing methods were developed during the 1930s, chrome and plastics like Bakelite replaced silver and ivory in production, making these versions less valuable today than the originals. On the other hand, Bakelite is collectible in its own right because it was used for many years to make a variety of household items.

Finally, be sure to watch out for reproductions and fakes. There are plenty of both out there, and collectors' guides usually include tips on how to spot one. There's nothing wrong with buying a reproduction if you like the piece, of course. Just don't pay the price of an original. The point is merely to know what you're buying.

New Ways to Find Old Things

One of the best ways to grow your collection is to put the word out to your friends. Anytime I've mentioned to someone that I collect Snoopy items, within a week they've brought me something. I've told so many of my friends that now they help me add to my collection fairly regularly (and of course I do the same for them). Fifty cents or a couple of dollars is no big deal to spend on the spur of the moment. A friend of mine who shall remain nameless once found me a Snoopy hand puppet in the donation box of an Alcoholics Anonymous meeting. (I'm not suggesting you do this. However, she did replace it with a stuffed animal.)

Another way to spread the word is to tell the parents of your children's friends at school. There's always some sort of parent-teacher night or class performance you can go to where you're sure to meet other parents. Time and time again, as my kids have changed schools, I start talking about my passion, and suddenly half the moms are on the lookout for Snoopy. Along with adding to my Snoopy collection, I've added some new friends to my life.

If you're collecting just for fun, you might be content to catch new pieces as you can at garage sales. But if you're collecting more seriously, reference books and publications should become a regular part of your reading. The more you're into collecting, the more you'll want to learn any-

Tip!

Bakelite is a whitish to reddish molding plastic that was widespread and popular in the 1930s and 1940s when it was used for a variety of household items like kitchenware, jewelry, and radios. You can tell Bakelite from other types of plastic by rubbing a piece hard and fast between your fingers until it heats up. Then smell it. If it smells like an old vacuum tube radio — that is, musty and electrical — it's Bakelite.

Garage Sale Gourmet

way. Subscribe to periodicals about antiques and collectibles to learn about current markets. Many of these, like *Antique Journal* and *West Coast Peddler*, are local or regional, so you can find out what's going on in your own area. And like I said, there are zillions of collectibles websites with all kinds of references, guides, online auctions, and other resources.

If you live in the city or a town with a lot of foot traffic, plan a garage saling expedition to the outskirts of your city and the surrounding suburbs. Chances are that you'll find collectibles cheaper than downtown, partly because there's less drive-by or foot traffic, which means sellers tend to be more willing to lower their prices for the few who do come along. Be sure to visit the upscale parts of town. People are likely to be selling nice things, and prices can be surprisingly low since they're selling more to get rid of things than to make a lot of money.

To track down pieces that are really hard to find, try researching the company that made them and find out when and where the pieces were originally sold. Then go to garage sales in those areas if you can. Start by looking on the item itself for a manufacturer's name. If you can't see a name, go through reference books looking for items like yours. Even if the line is no longer being produced, the company may still be around and is likely to have records of where the merchandise was distributed — possibly by state or county and maybe by individual store location. Try the community relations department; it's likely to be more helpful in tracking down information than the customer service department. Collectibles websites may contain information on an elusive company or product, and you can contact other collectors through online communities and newsgroups to ask questions.

Possibly your particular set or style was sold through certain department stores. You can find a directory of current store locations on a chain's website and contact the community relations office to find out where — and maybe when — other stores were closed.

If a store or manufacturer is no longer in business, there may be articles of incorporation or Chapter 11 bankruptcy filings on file with the secretary of state. You might also check with the department of corporations where the company was incorporated, if you can find that out. These files are public records, and you should be able to get them for the price of photocopies or search for them on your state's official website.

How badly you want to find something will determine how much time and effort you're willing to put into it. If you're persevering and patient, the rewards could be well worth it. The more you research and the more you see out there — once you get familiar with a style, you'll start seeing it everywhere — the more exciting it gets.

In this chapter

7

The Big Score

The common dream of every garage saler is the big score. Sometimes you get lucky and find money or even jewelry in the pocket of a coat or bottom of a handbag. Or you might pay $5 for a cute little statuette or a box of "cheap" jewelry only to discover that the figure is a Hummel, or that some of the rings are signed and valuable. I once found a sterling silver bracelet in the top drawer of a desk. Now I have both a nice bracelet and a great story.

Garage saling is often like that, but unfortunately you can't count on it, much less plan for it. You can, however, plan for even bigger scores, and that gets us to the heart of being a garage sale gourmet: It's about making small improvements in your life every day, both financially and creatively.

Once you've bought something at a garage sale, there are two things you can do: keep it or sell it.

Many people shop at garage sales to make money by re-selling their purchases. Online auctions like eBay have only gotten more popular, and there are now several good books on how to buy and sell online. You can also sell through traditional venues like classified ads. We're here to talk about garage sales, though, and about how to hold your own, now that you've seen everybody else's. What online auctions can't replace is the tangible experience of the garage sale itself: the feel and smell of things, the thrill of being out shopping, and, not least, the pleasure of real human interaction.

I've held many garage sales, but my main reason for garage saling is to keep what I buy and use it creatively to create a nice home without paying department store prices. My big score is that I get to experience the results of my garage saling every day, every time I sit at my dining table or open my living room drapes, and feel like, "I did this!" That's a feeling you can't find in any pricing guide.

Holding Your Own Garage Sale

You buy to resell for one reason — to make money. Furniture in particular has a high resale value, if you want to invest the time and energy to fix and refinish it. But you can also stockpile and resell clothing, collectibles, appliances, sporting goods, and many other types of items. With enough of something, you can highlight your specialty in a classified ad and attract people with a serious interest. On the other hand, you may just want to hold a sale to clear your home after doing the home inventory in chapter 1, so you can make room and raise money for the items on your shopping list.

If you want to pursue garage saling so you can resell, consider a few things:

1. You have to be willing to go out there with a purpose every weekend, or close to it, in order to amass enough stuff so that your markup adds up to something. You may enjoy garage saling every weekend, but it'll feel more like work, and you'll be self-imposing pressure to get good deals.

2. You'll want to get to sales early on Saturday, to snap up the good stuff, or late on Sunday, when people really start marking things down, so mapping out your days by time rather than location may make more sense.

3. You may be limited to how many garage sales you can hold. In some cities, if you hold a garage sale more than twice a year, it's considered a small business. That means you'll have to get a business license and pay taxes on your income — or face back taxes plus fines if you get caught.

Whatever your reason, do something to elevate your garage sale above the rest. The sale may be outside, but in a way it's still like inviting people into your home: they come to visit, they see what you have. If you think of it that way, instead of merely as a sale, you can create a shopping experience that will earn you more money because people will feel more at home buying from you.

Planning Your Sale
You go out to all these garage sales and think it's so easy... until you organize your own.

Prepare your sale a month in advance, but if you shop to resell, then set up a place in your home where you can store and refinish your purchases on an ongoing basis. That way you won't keep things scattered around the house for months and then have to rush to find and fix everything the week before your sale.

When you actually start planning, the first thing to do is write down, off the top of your head, a list of all the things you've liked and disliked about other people's sales. Were prices marked, or did you always have to ask? Could you figure out who to pay? Were items laid out with any organization or just scattered around? Were the sellers friendly, or did they pretty much ignore you? As you go out yard saling, keep notes on what others do that's catchy or effective and what you swear you'll never do if you ever hold your own sale.

Consider when to hold your sale. Many people think a three-day holiday weekend is a good time, but I don't.

Locals tend to be out of town, so you actually get fewer people driving by. Also, when you're planning your own garage saling expeditions, you'll notice which day or days other people hold sales in your area. In Los Angeles, most sales are on Saturday, so if I plan mine for Sunday and then advertise it, I'm likely to get a better turnout.

Make it a part of your routine, when you're at a sale, to ask other shoppers how they heard about it. This will now suggest to you some effective ways to publicize your own sale.

Think about parking. I went to a sale in an alley, and there was absolutely no place to park nearby. It was on a hill in a permit only zone. How frustrating is that? People got fed up and drove away. If you want people to come to your sale, help them with parking. If you're on or near an alley, or parking in your neighborhood is tight, find areas to park nearby and post signs with directions to them in front of your sale. If your block has permit only parking, call or visit your city hall (try the parking and traffic department) and ask for a supply of one-day parking permits. On sale day, have a friend or family member stand at the curb and hand them out to interested customers who drive by. I did this once, and our local parking meter guy loved it because it made his job easier. Our customers thanked us too.

Signs

Signs are crucial. After Saturday morning, signs are almost the only way people will find out about your sale.

This may sound obvious, but for some reason it doesn't seem to be: Write your address BIG. Most of the time, sellers write GARAGE SALE large and visibly and the address small, so that by the time you even see the address, you've driven past the sign. I can't tell you how many addresses — and sales — I have missed this way.

Don't post signs only at the end of your block. Give drivers time to turn down your street by posting signs like this one block before the turn: "Garage Sale, Next Right." Then they're ready for the sign on your corner with the address written BIG. Arrows are helpful, but don't draw arrows on your signs until you've posted them so you can make sure they point in the right direction.

> **Tip!**
>
> Piggyback your signs near other yard sales. For garage sale junkies like me, it gets our hearts pumping to see all those signs and sales together. Find other sales by checking the ads for the weekend of your sale, then head out the evening before and put your signs a house or two down the block from the other sales so that shoppers won't miss them.

Give the hours of the sale. If you open an hour earlier or stay open an hour later than the other sales in your neighborhood, you give yourself some time to attract customers without competition.

Finally, don't forget to take down your signs after the sale. Some cities will cite you for leaving them up, and you're easy for cops to find because, duh, the sign gives your address. Even if you don't get fined, you'll be sleeping in the next day and someone who didn't pay attention to the date will show up at your door at seven o'clock. You only need this to happen once and you'll swear never to leave your signs up after a sale again.

Setting Up the Space

Most people holding yard sales scatter their stuff around with little or no thought to how it's arranged, other than spreading it out so everything can be seen. B-o-o-o-ring. Take the time to create a nice display. This is the one part of your planning that customers will actually see. It's their first impression, the one that will stay with them.

To be a good seller, use your shopping experience. Think back to your list of likes and dislikes and create the kind of garage sale you would want to shop at. Which displays were most effective or attracted your attention? How effective were the signs in getting you there? If the sale was advertised, how did the ad compare with reality? How was traffic flow managed? Were some items hard to reach? Could you easily find the person with the cash box?

If you have enough different kinds of items, consider setting up your sale area like a department store, with old blankets laid out to mark off different "departments." Post a sign by each one: Housewares, Clothing, Sports Equipment, etc. Make a separate Toys & Games department so that kids will have a space to play and keep out of the way. They'll have an easier time finding something to buy than if the playthings are mixed in with everything else.

If you really want to sell a particular item, put it out front and on display. I mean really on display, like at the curb. This is a common technique that I mentioned earlier, but go one step further by helping your potential buyers visualize the item completely. I once put a complete dining room set on my lawn, with placemats and napkin rings on the table and a rug underneath it, and a woman bought the whole thing because she could picture how it would look in her home.

If you have a lot of furniture, put out what you can, then print out digital photos of the rest and display them in your furniture department with prices. That way, if someone is really interested, you can take them inside to see the pieces in their actual setting. This beats putting up a "More Furniture Inside" sign and having herds of mere lookers tromp through your home.

If you have a lot of clothing, it's better to use hangers than to pile it on the ground, where it'll get all messed up by people scrounging through it carelessly. Those space-saver units designed for closets can be pulled out, in whole or part, to make free-standing clothing racks for the lawn or driveway. Or run a thin rope or cord through a length of plastic pipe (PVC is available at hardware stores) and string it up between two trees. The light tubing makes a perfect rack that won't snag hangers or sag in the middle like cord alone would do.

If you are selling drapes, you can do something similar by tying up a curtain rod between two trees. Hang sheers (which are light) on a length of fishing line or twine so people see only the drapes themselves. It's a pain to keep unfolding and refolding curtains, blankets, and table-cloths, so leave them folded and write the dimensions on the price tag. (Someone will unfold them anyway, but you knew that.)

When you did your comparison shopping to establish price ranges in chapter 5, you learned how much you should expect to pay for things, but you also learned the reverse: how much you can get. But don't think you'll be clever by pricing items to end in .95 and .99. We're used to it in retail stores, but at garage sales it's annoying. Not only won't shoppers like the obvious trick, but it complicates making change when someone makes a purchase. If you price things only at even dollar amounts — or amounts ending in .25, .50, or .75 — then you never need any change on hand except quarters, and there's less chance of making mistakes.

Set up a table that's clearly the "cash register." Naturally, someone will do exactly what I urged you not to do earlier, namely bargain you down to two dollars and then pay with a $20 bill. But you can handle it, because you'll be prepared with lots of ones and fives and coins. Get a cash box or a partitioned cash wallet like waitresses use or some other system to keep organized. Buy a pad of receipts at your local office supply store and have several pens handy. Keep a stack of grocery bags (paper and plastic) at the register, and maybe a couple of boxes, for all those poor folks who didn't read this book and so forgot to bring their own bags. Do not leave your cash box lying around on a table, for obvious reasons. Get a length of sturdy cord or wire and tie the cash box handle to one of the table's legs. Keep the box locked.

Tip!

Place a large mirror at the curb. Not only will it attract attention, but people can use it for trying on clothing.

Finally, get your family involved. Don't stick your kids in front of the TV or ship them to a friend's house. Let them help. Give them assignments, and you'll be amazed at how many people will buy from them. Everyone loves a child entrepreneur. At one of my yard sales, we filled an airpot with coffee, put bottled water in a cooler, and put out some donuts. There's no profit in donuts, but we struck gold with the water, and the coffee was a bonus that the early morning shoppers really appreciated. My son Alex is old enough to handle cash, and Chloe, who was six at the time, paraded up and down the sidewalk with a sign like she was a ring girl. We were in hysterics, and so were our buyers. The kids had a blast and even made some money by selling their Pokemon cards and toys. We put a cup in front of them at the cash register table that read College Fund. Just make sure you spell college right.

Becoming a Garage Sale Gourmet

If I were in a contest or on a show like *Trading Spaces*, sure, I could redecorate my home in a weekend, if I also had a crew and a limitless budget. But that's not how life really works. Not mine, anyway. Instead, I redecorate a little bit at a time in an ongoing fashion, rather than all at once. That way, doing something to beautify my home and enjoying that experience become a small but steady part of everyday life. This is the essence of being a garage sale gourmet.

Tip!

If you're selling shoes, set up a bench or some chairs or stools so people can sit to try them on.

People don't come into my house and think almost everything is from garage sales, even though it is. What I do is mix inexpensive pieces with more expensive ones, choosing one or two big-ticket items — a bed or sofa, for example — as the pieces I want to last while I decorate around them with garage sale buys, which I can change whenever I like. Because I'm good at bargain shopping and at mixing old and new items, I can buy a lot of things with relatively little money, which lets me save for the pricier things.

As you're doing your home inventory, think about the one or two big-ticket items you might like to have for each room, and then plan to get everything else at garage sales. Of course, you can do all this without buying any expensive pieces at all, and shop garage sales for everything. But maybe you want your child's room to have a big, solid bed that will last until college. Or maybe he or she is older and really needs a bigger desk for studies and a computer station, and a modest bed will do for the next few years. Good furniture is more like an investment than most other home decorations. For things like desk lamps, toys, nightstands, decorative baskets, pillows, and so forth, there's no reason to spend a fortune if you don't have to.

Tip!

Make sure that sizes are marked on clothing. Even though size is not a good fitting guide for secondhand clothing, people still like to know.

You can approach your shopping from either direction, either beginning or ending with the big-ticket item. If you know there's an expensive piece that you want to ground a room and last for a while — a bed, say, or a dining room set or sofa (see sidebar "My Living Room") — then buy that first and decorate around it. Or, set yourself up with a budget of a couple hundred dollars and buy the inexpensive furnishings first — a dresser, shelves, chairs, and so forth — and then use the savings to buy the nice, expensive piece you have in mind to bring it all together when you're ready, or when you find it.

Look at it this way: you can make cheap mistakes or expensive mistakes. If you find a table lamp you like at a garage sale but it doesn't look so good in your home after all, don't agonize over it; you only spent ten bucks. Get rid of it at your own garage sale. By hitting the sales each weekend, you'll find something you like better, and probably for less. When you find it, you won't feel so guilty about buying it because you hardly spent anything for the first one. With garage sales, it's easy to explore your personal taste and style this way — something you probably wouldn't do if you had to pay full retail price for everything.

Turning Garbage into Gold

An important thing to remember when you're planning your spaces is that you don't have to use everything from garage sales "as is," but you can alter items to suit your needs. With basic materials like fabric and paint and a handful of ordinary supplies — a stapler, screwdrivers, needles and thread, scissors, epoxy, nails, sandpaper, and putty — pretty much anybody can undertake basic repairs or refinishing that will pay off beautifully.

Tip!

If you're selling jewelry, don't just throw it all into a box. Even costume jewelry will look nicer, and pricier, if you polish it and lay it out on towels or sweaters for display. If you crinkle up the material a bit, you'll get a nicely textured showroom effect.

At a garage sale, you could be staring at exactly what you want and not know it. You just need to see beyond first impressions. If you find a piece that's close, imagine it in your home where you'd want it, but perhaps in a different color, or with new drawer knobs or whatever. We talked about this at the beginning of chapter 4 — the third key thing to remember. Don't be discouraged if the only thing wrong with those perfect bar stools is the wrong color of seat fabric, because you don't need to find a red chair if you can buy a blue one and recover it. Just undo the handful of screws underneath the seat, remove the fabric, cut another piece of the same size in the material you want, and refasten it over the original padding. A beat-up-looking dresser that's not falling apart can return to brilliance with sandpaper, a quart of paint, and a couple hours of your time.

We also talked about taking into account the necessary or desirable cost of repairs or refinishing when you consider whether to spend the money for a reasonably suitable piece. A wrought iron candle holder I bought for four dollars was worth it because it needed only a spot weld. Had it been badly damaged or rusted, needing more extensive repair, I'd have been better off letting it go. Instead, I took it to an industrial welding shop that fixed it in half an hour for ten dollars. A candelabra repair shop would have cost much more, and they'd probably have sent it to a professional welder anyway. Spending $10 to fix a $4 item sounds silly at first, but I look at it this way: for only $14 I got a candle holder that I really love, that I can use outdoors to add an intimate, candlelit touch to garden parties.

Tip!

Colored dot labels for marking prices are easy to see and come off easily, but if you have a certain type of item in abundance, like children's toys, consider dumping them into one box or grab bag and selling the whole thing for $5. Or post a sign that says, "Any item 25¢." This total price approach lets you get rid of the entire lot easily. Remember, just like anyone holding a garage sale, you don't want to have to store all this stuff again.

More Design Ideas

I prefer to spend the big money on big items I want to last a while, so the garage sale buys can be the accessories and

My Living Room

My living room is a good example of how I mix big-ticket items with garage sale buys to turn a room into a comfortable, livable space. My husband and I wanted a really nice, big, plush, L-shaped sofa and ended up spending more than we anticipated to have it custom built because we couldn't find the one we wanted in any store. That was the item we wanted as the centerpiece, to ground the room and set the tone. We also spent a couple hundred on a huge, carved wooden coffee table that will outlast us all.

We didn't buy drapes because I can sew. I bought curtain rods with finials and tiebacks at an ironwork shop for the overstock price of five dollars a set. To my advantage, they goofed because there were actually two sets per box, not one, so my good deal got doubled. I then found some chenille fabric that was the exact color of the sofa. I knew it was exact because I carry swatches of my furniture fabrics to sales and pretty much everywhere I go. I never know where I'll end up. Chenille is expensive — $60 a yard — but I got a special deal because there were only eight yards left, the last of the bolt. I got all of it for $60. I just love when that happens. Because I got the rods and fabric so cheaply, I told myself I could splurge for some expensive silk to make sheers for the perfect finishing touch, but even so, I was spending less than new drapes would cost.

The rest of the room is decorated with baskets, throw pillows, candle holders and a mixture of other decorative pieces, most of which I bought in that incredible big score the weekend of Chloe's birthday party — in chapter 4, remember?

In other words, we spent the big money on two major pieces (the sofa and coffee table), but spent only a couple hundred dollars on the rest of the room combined, mostly on decorative pieces that I can replace at any time and not worry about cost, because I can get it all at garage sales.

fun stuff. That way, I can change my decor by replacing just a handful of items instead of doing an entire makeover. My living room design is based on the sofa and drapes, but I could change the entire look of the room with new pillow slipcovers and throw blankets, different colored candles, or small tables in place of the baskets. Since most of my furniture

Tip!

The welder who fixed my candle holder also repaired my patio furniture, so I can get many more years out of that too for a small investment.

is neutral in color, I have wide latitude in choosing new paint for the walls to give any room a whole new look, or I could leave the walls alone and repaint the furniture.

My dining room furniture consists of an oval table and chairs that I bought at different garage sales and painted an antiqued white, as well as a glass-fronted cabinet made of two stacked pieces, which I also bought at separate sales but painted a glossy white. With these as my foundation pieces, I can give the room all kinds of looks. Its everyday color scheme is yellow, which I achieve with a combination of effects: mustard-colored walls, matching seat covers I made in much the way I described replacing a bar stool seat, a gold fabric sash laid diagonally across the table, and the decorative knickknacks I display in the cabinet.

The cabinet is where the power of collections shows itself. Some of the pieces in it get used, like place settings, but some of them are just decorative: vases, candles, colorful salt and pepper shakers, and so on. The connection is that almost all of them are or contain yellow, from the bright yellow shakers to the yellow rim of the dinner plates. It doesn't matter that the yellows aren't all exactly the same; the look is unified. To alter the room completely, I'd only need to repaint the walls (say, blue), recover the seats, and replace the sash and cabinet items with blue ones, which at garage sales is easy to do.

I can also change the room's look on a smaller scale for special occasions. Obviously I'm not going to repaint the room and replace everything for every holiday, but because the furniture is neutral, I can bring out my red table settings for a red-and-gold Christmas look that's not kitschy, or blue settings for Hanukah, or purple for Easter (we celebrate a lot of things here). Where did I get all these decorations and place settings? Garage sales, of course. You'll be surprised to see how much a little bit of playing with color like this can change the look of a room.

In other words, garage sale shopping makes it easy to change your mind without a great deal of hassle.

Tip!

Display your collections. That's what they're for. If you have lots of pieces, don't feel like you have to display them all. They'll be too crowded to show off properly and will just collect dust because you'll never feel like doing that much cleaning all at once. It's better to display a few pieces, but nicely, and maybe rotate them with pieces stored in your closet so there's always something new to look at and enjoy. Obviously I can't display all three thousand of my Snoopy collectibles, but I keep enough pieces displayed in different rooms so that it's clear to anyone visiting that someone in the house really likes Snoopy.

It also makes it easy to be ready for any occasion without

spending lots of money. What's not to like about this? Shopping at garage sales gives you flexibility because it costs so little to experiment. It makes home decorating a fun and creative experience.

The Big Score

Look where we've been.

You've taken inventory, gotten your garage saling kit together, mapped out your day, done research, bargained some good deals, started a collection, and begun to beautify your home. Wow! Once you're doing this regularly, it'll become habit — more than that, part of the way you live. I walk around all the time with swatches of fabric and paint because I never know when I'll be driving around and see a sign...

Being a garage sale gourmet means you don't have to "design down" to fit your budget. You can design your home with the same flair as if you were spending a lot. Garage saling is not just about shopping, but about making your home nicer on an ongoing basis. It doesn't matter if you live with your family in a two-story home, alone in a one-room apartment, or anywhere in between.

Garage saling is like going on a treasure hunt every weekend, knowing there's treasure everywhere. It's about fun and serendipity, about getting out in your neighborhood, about the excitement of the unknown, and the thrill of getting a good deal. And it's about personal creativity, about making your living environment into some-thing beautiful, and feeling a sense of accomplishment and satisfaction.

I can't think of any bigger score than that.

In this appendix

Garage Sales and Resale Shops

Supplies

Mapping Websites

Collectibles and Antiques

Books and Publishers

Design and Decor

Appendix A

Going Further: Additional Resources

Garage Sales and Resale Shops

- *The Pocket Idiot's Guide to Garage and Yard Sales*, by Cathy Pedigo and Sonia Weiss (2003, Alpha Books, 184 pages)

  There are several books available on Amazon.com that are guides to holding a garage sale, but I'm including here the two I liked best. This is one. It's comprehensive and systematic, knowledgeable and well written. You'll feel like you've covered everything when you're done.

- *The Backyard Money Machine*, by Les Schmeltz (1993, Silver Streak Publications, 220 pages)
  This is the other one. Very detailed and useful. You'll feel like you've covered everything and then some.

- Yard Sale Queen *www.yardsalequeen.com*
  A fun and useful website with lots of information for holding as well as shopping at garage sales, including tips, stories, links to other yard sale websites, and more.

- National Association of Resale and Thrift Shops *www.narts.org*
  The handy thing about the NARTS website is the searchable database of its members, so you can locate thrift and consignment stores all over the country.

Supplies

- SplashData *www.splashdata.com*
  This company makes good, inexpensive applications for PDAs and cell phones that let you create and synchronize shopping lists and digital photos.

- DataViz *www.dataviz.com*
  Maker of the Documents To Go spreadsheet and word processing application for PDAs.

- Garage Sale Supplies *www.salesigns.info*
  Garage sale signs and labels for sale, if for some reason you feel you need to spend money on these things.

Mapping Websites

Mapping sites have gotten much better over the years, more able to produce maps in the way most people use and want them: to go. You can print each map with directions or download them to your PDA for taking on the road.

- MapQuest *www.mapquest.com*
- Yahoo! Maps *maps.yahoo.com*
- MSN Maps *maps.msn.com*
- Rand McNally *www.randmcnally.com*

Collectibles and Antiques

- About.com *collectibles.about.com*
  Website with a lot of basic information about collectibles and links to online pricing guides, useful articles, and more.

- Antiques Roadshow *www.antiquesroadshow.com*
  Official website of the popular PBS TV show.

- Collect.com *www.collect.com*
  The online collecting community of Krause Publications (see the next section, "Books and Publishers").

- Curioscape *www.curioscape.com*
  A directory/portal site with scores of links to other collectibles websites.

- West Coast Peddler *westcoastpeddler.com*
  One of the leading publications on the West Coast, with news, show ads and listings, informational articles, and more.

- Journal of Antiques and Collectibles
  www.journalofantiques.com
  The website of the print magazine includes a calendar of antique shows and flea markets around the country as well as selected articles from past issues and other useful links.

- Replacements.com *www.replacements.com*
  Not really a collectibles website, but a site where you can buy replacements for almost every imaginable household item, including collectibles, which means it's good for researching their market prices.

Books and Publishers

- *Treasures in Your Attic*, by Joe L. Rosson and Helaine Fendelman (2001, Harper Collins, 352 pages)
  If you're serious about becoming a collector, start with this excellent introduction to the art and science of antiques and collectibles and to finding them where you live. Written by the hosts of the TV show with the same name, it starts by setting you straight on the difference between what is collectible or valuable and what you only think is collectible or valuable, then takes you on a tour of your own home to see what's really there. Good for doing that collectibles inventory in chapter 6.

- Carter's American Junk *www.carterjunk.com*
  The author of the Junk Books series — *Garden Junk*, *Kitchen Junk*, and *Big City Junk* — talks about collecting and decorating using finds from sidewalk sales and flea markets, with lots of photos and stories of her junking expeditions.

- Kovels *www.kovels.com*
  Kovels publishes about a dozen books on collectibles and antiques, and its website includes articles, links, and other information in addition to selling the books. *Know Your Collectibles* is an excellent place to start for new collectors. It's full of illustrations, photos, manufacturers' marks to help you identify pieces,

and lots of information — especially about pottery, jewelry, and glass, but toys, lamps, clocks, and other categories have chapters too.

- Schiffer Publishing *www.schifferbooks.com*
  Schiffer publishes hundreds of heavily illustrated books about collectibles. The site is mostly a catalogue of its publications with not much in the way of information, but if a book is what you want to find, look here.

- GemStone Press *www.gemstonepress.com*
  This publisher focuses exclusively on gemstones and jewelry, but it doesn't sell just books. You can also buy loupes, spectroscopes, refractometers, and other equipment to help you tell gems from glass.

- Krause Publications *www.krause.com*
  Publisher of eight periodicals (including *Antique Journal*) and a large line of books about antiques. Its Collect.com community website is a treasure trove of news, dealer directories, and other information about antiques and collectibles.

- Collector Books *www.collectorbooks.com*
  Publishes dozens of books about collectibles that feature lots of full-color photos.

- House of Collectibles *www.houseofcollectibles.com*
  The website of Random House's line of collectibles

guides, including the Instant Expert series for beginners, covering broad categories like books, Art Deco, and oriental rugs.

Design and Decor

- Home & Garden Television *www.hgtv.com*.
  Website of the television network. A cornucopia of great decorating and landscaping ideas.

- *Secondhand Chic: Finding Fabulous Fashion at Consignment, Vintage, and Thrift Stores*, by Christa Weil (1999, Pocket Books, 328 pages)
  This book got my brother, co-author Randy, who has no interest whatsoever in fashion or clothing design, interested in fashion and clothing design. He says that's how good it is, although he doesn't dress any differently. If you want to learn how clothes are made, how they should fit, how they are sold in the thrift shop/resale market, or how to design your wardrobe, Weil can tell you anything you could think of to ask.

- *The Garage Sale Decorator's Bible*, by Shelley Kincaid (1997, Shelley Kincaid, 293 pages)
  This book covers in great detail the inventive things you can do with your garage sale finds, from repairing and decorating them to using them in creative and sometimes unexpected ways.

In this appendix

Car Supplies

Field Supplies

Packing Supplies

Appendix B

Garage Saling Supplies Checklist

For quick reference, here is a checklist of garage saling supplies from chapter 3. For more supplies and resources, visit www.garagesalegourmet.com.

Car Supplies

- Food and water
- Maps
- Umbrella/extra weather appropriate clothing

Field Supplies

- Tape measure
- Magnifying glass/jeweler's loupe
- Flashlight
- Black light (for ceramics and porcelain)
- Batteries/extension cord
- Pen and paper
- Coin purse/change
- Camera (digital, cell phone, PDA)
- Instant handle
- Reference books

Packing Supplies

- Scissors
- Wrapping material (newspaper, bubble wrap)
- Boxes
- Packing tape
- Plastic bags
- Casters (for furniture)
- Padding
- Ropes, ties, straps

Garage Sale Gourmet

Index

G

Glassware
 boxes for, 54–55
 checking for chips on, 71
Government
 involvement in sales, 35–36
 regulation of sales, 4–5, 103

H

Handles, instant, 53
Holding sales, 102–110
 planning for, 104–105
 reasons for, 102–104
 regulations on, 4–5, 103
 setting up for, 107–110
 signs for, 105–107
Household items, shopping for, 67–70
Hunchback position, 1

I

Internet
 collectibles on, information on, 91, 123–124
 finding sales on, 33–34, 35
 list of useful sites, 121–127
 research on, 80–81, 97–98
 shopping on, 10
Intimidation, 32–33
Inventory
 of collections, 90–91
 of needs, 18–21

J

Jewelry
 selling, 113
 shopping for, 50, 69

Newsletters, finding sales in, 35
Newspapers, finding sales in, 34–37

O
Online. *See* Internet
Optimism, 70–72
Orange County (California), 38

P
Packing supplies, 54–56, 130
Padding, 55
Painting walls, 21
Paper, 51
Parents, working, characteristics of, 8
Parking, 105
Partial payments, 28–29
PDAs, 25, 52–53
Pencils, 51
Pens, 51
Periodicals, 22, 25, 97
Photographs, 25
Planning, 31–42
    finding sales, 33–37
    mapping sales, 38–42
Plastic bags, 55
Porcelain, supplies for shopping for, 50, 51
Position, hunchback, 1
Price labels
    finding chips underneath, 65
    removing, 70
    using colored dots as, 114
Prices
    conventional wisdom on, 63, 81
    evaluating, 62–63
    negotiating
        misconceptions about, 11–12
        tips on, 64–67

W

Walls, painting, 21
Water, 48
Welding, 114, 116
West Coast Peddler (periodical), 97, 124
Wooden items, termite dust on, 93
Working parents, characteristics of, 8
Wrapping material, 54
Writing shopping lists, 23–26

About the Authors

Anita Chagaris and Randy Lyman are a sister and brother with more than thirty years' combined experience in writing and garage sale shopping. Anita, the shopper, lives in Santa Monica, California, with her husband and two rapidly growing children. Randy, the writer, lives farther north, in Oakland, and has worked as a journalist, editor, travel writer, translator, publicist, poet, or whatever else was needed at the time.

Garage Sale Gourmet

is available online
or at your favorite bookstore.
Quantity discounts are available to
qualifying institutions.

Garage Sale Gourmet is distributed by
Independent Publishers Group. Visit
www.ipgbook.com for more information.
Available to the booktrade and educators
through all major wholesalers.

For more information, visit
www.GarageSaleGourmet.com
or contact Fighting Words Press at
P.O. Box 1041, Oakland, CA 94604

Fighting
Words Press